Lu Xun Prize Win:

Zhang Yawen's

Battle for Life

ISSN 2332-4287 (print); ISSN 2334-1122 (online)

Chinese Literature and Culture
www.clcjournal.com
Volume 8, December, 2016

Editor-in-Chief
Chu Dongwei
Guangdong University of Foreign Studies

New Leaves®

Jointly published in the United States by IntLingo Inc., Westbury, New York & Zilin Limited, Guangzhou. New Leaves® is a US imprint and trademark of Zilin Cultural Development Company Limited Guangzhou.

PLEASE CONNECT WITH US ON FACEBOOK:
https://www.facebook.com/clcjournal

Praises for Zhang Yawen and her works:

Zhang Yawen excels in fiction, non-fiction, and screenwriting, an incredible achievement in itself, not to say that such an outstanding achievement comes from a woman writer who has had only five years of school. The many misfortunes of her life have turned into a bleak yet rigorous light of reason in her works.

Wu Jingquan & Wang Xiuchen
Harbin Normal University

The Call of Life [also translated as *Cry for Life*], deserves to be recommended to our families and our children for its value as a family treasure book. It teaches how the flower of dignity grows in adversity, against rain, snow, sleet, and frost, and gives us an understanding of what constitutes a beautiful feeling and a beautiful marriage, and of the charm of pursuing a goal, having family, being loyal to loved ones, and hoping...

Chen Jiangong, writer

A good autobiography must be complete with three elements: a story, skill to tell a story, and ability to touch the reader. Zhang Yawen has done it and has done it remarkably well.

Zhao Baisheng, Peking University

Playing Games with the Devil is unique by standing out in perspective, insight, character delineation, and temporal and spatial arrangements...It shines with the light of humanism and peace, and the greatness of humanity...

Lei Da
critic

Contributing Editors of Volume 8:

Fraser Sutherland
Canadian author and poet

Craig Hulst
Grand Valley State University

Contributors:
Chu Dongwei, Zhang Yawen, Ying Kong

Translators:

Chu Dongwei, Ying Kong, Vincent Dong, Tina Sim

Cover photo of author Zhang Yawen: courtesy of Zhang Yawen

Contents

Editorial: Zhang Yawen's Battle for Life

By Chu Dongwei, Editor in Chief

Perhaps the best way to celebrate life is to fight for it.

There is so much in life and there is so much to say, and here we are lucky to be involved with a writer who is filled with the zest for life and is never tired of telling its stories.

A seventy-something? Yes, she is. Yet when it comes to telling life's stories, she tells them like a seven year old, with as much excitement, without guile, and yet one cannot help being affected. And you feel she is telling your stories and they happened yesterday.

I am not unfamiliar with the surroundings in which Yawen grew up. The bigger story repeats itself though the individual stories that make up the bigger story differ from person to person in spite of the varying milieus.

Life is a gift and the gift should be appreciated. Very often a person specially gifted meets with greater adversity in her life and it takes courage and perseverance and skill to overcome it. It is the sense of mission that sets apart an individual from a crowd that can be unconscious, insensitive, or maddening. In a word, one needs to know what she is doing.

In this volume, we have a short sketch "First Love at a Deathbed," a pathetic story of Yawen's Third Elder Sister regretting not having fought for her own life on her deathbed. "Dog Girl" is Ying Kong's English adaptation of excerpts of Yawen's early fight against fate in getting her limited education. "The Hawthorn Tree at the Beginning of My Life," translated by the smiling but serious translator Tina Sim, documents the hard life of the family in a valley with its suppressed aspirations and feelings. "In Respect and Awe" is Vincent Dong's translation of Yawen's preface to her prize-winning biographical novel *Playing Games with the Devil*, for the writing of which she made many interview trips to Europe on her own. In "Zhang Yawen's Calling: Rising Against All Odds," Ying Kong gives an in-depth introduction to the Lu Xun Prize winning autobiography *The Call of Life* (translated as *Cry for Life* in an existing English translation) with a poetic summary of the author's life in the first person singular.

Besides all the people mentioned above, a special

thank you goes to Canadian author Fraser Sutherland who spent the Christmas holidays reading and editing all the translations with me, over the Internet. CLC's long-time friend Craig Hulst has helped endorse sample translations.

Thanks to the participating scholars and translators, 2016 saw steady development of CLC, which can now be discovered in EBSCOhost's two databases: *Humanities Source Ultimate collection* and *One Belt, One Road Reference Source* collection, and is offered as a subscription journal through the Editorial Office and designated distributors and electronically across devices--computers, mobile phones, and tablets--through online newsstand portal Magzter in addition to its availability as a book series in the major online bookstores.

We will welcome our tenth volume in mid-2017. In the twinkling of an eye, to use a cliché, it is the fourth year since the conception of CLC. If we don't try it, we never know what we can do.

First Love at a Deathbed

by Zhang Yawen, translated by Chu Dongwei

I wondered if it was my last time to see *Sanjie*, Third Elder Sister.

She was seriously ill and I returned to my hometown to see her. She lay in bed, the way my mother did before dying, attached to the bed like a flat, withered leaf devoid of previous stamina and vigor. However, *Sanjie* only made it to 60 and my mother died at age 89.

"Sanjie," I called, tears rolling down my eyes, wondering if she still remembered me.

She stared at me for a long while with her languid eyes and suddenly called out, "Yawen!" And then she cried like a baby, her mouth open wide. Her cry of grievance and catharsis tore at the heart of a sister bound by blood and ripped open a life of misery...

Sanjie's life had been unfortunate. She was not alone. All my three elder sisters had been unfortunate, *Dajie* —

Eldest Sister — and *Erjie* — Second Elder Sister — having never attended school for a single day, *Erjie* dead at 24 and *Dajie* scratching out an unmemorable existence.

Having only had two years of school, Sanjie became an apprentice in a factory very early in her life. Later, through the introduction of an acquaintance, she married a talented university graduate, an engineer of the Shijingshan Iron and Steel Plant in Beijing. However, the two had no common language due to the great educational gap. On top of that, most of the time they lived in different places, Sanjie struggling with life in a small Northern city raising two kids single-handed. What was worse, during the Cultural Revolution, her husband died an early death because of acute encephalitis. She later dated twice without success. She became more and more irritable, more and more difficult to get along with. Once I saw her leaning against the window and sighing to herself, "While all people are seen in pairs, why on earth is there no man for me?" As she turned around, I saw her eyes were full of tears. On another occasion, my husband and I went to visit her. Seeing the affection passing between us two, she said, out of the blue, "Yawen, you had an independent mind!"

When I fell in love with the boy, my father stubbornly objected, but I did not listen to him.

Holding her big rough hand, I consoled her for a long time before Sanjie's crying subsided. Nonetheless, she would not let the door be closed, shouting as she sobbed, "Liu Guanglai, come in! Take away the bedpan and get me a glass of water..." Poor Sanjie was suffering from auditory and visual hallucinations.

My niece told me that Sanjie had been calling out the name ever since she got sick and wondered who that man exactly was. I also wondered why Sanjie called out a stranger's name instead of the name of my brother-in-law. "Who's Liu Guanglai?" I asked.

She said, "He's from the Shenyang Military Region, large, tall, with big eyes ..." and then said, "Do you not agree to my dating him?"

I said, "Yes, I do, Sanjie. I give you my blessing."

Hearing that, Sanjie was satisfied and said, "Good, you agree. He's waiting for me at the door. I'll let him in and introduce him to you. Old Liu, come in please. Sis has agreed!"

There was not a single soul at the door, except for a

gust of cold wind.

Sanjie, however, pointed at the empty space and said in a serious voice, "Yawen, meet my beau Liu Guanglai. Isn't he handsome?"

Hah. I remembered. Way back in the early 1950s, when my family removed to Jiamusi City, a wounded soldier from the Korean war front stayed in a hospital not far from my home—a very handsome young man, it was—and often visited us, but my father stubbornly objected to the relationship and destroyed it.

Now, over half a century had passed and while the days of *Sanjie* were numbered she still cherished the memory of her first love. It was saddening indeed.

Seeing my tears, Sanjie stared at me blankly and asked, "Why do you cry? Don't you agree to my dating Liu Guanglai?"

I held her in my arms and cried out loud, "Sanjie!"

My poor third elder sister had been longing for a real relationship of love but didn't get it until she died.

These days, I have been thinking, if my father had not interfered in Sanjie's right to love, or if Sanjie had resolutely defended her right to love like me, what would have become of her now?

After all, there is no *if* in life but regrets.

Translated from

张雅文：临终前的初恋，《今晚报》，2009 年 11 月 16 日

The Chinese electronic text is provided by Zhang Yawen.

Dog Girl

from *The Call of Life*
by Zhang Yawen, translated by Ying Kong

The little girl had a beautiful dream, to return to the city where she would study, sing, and dance at school like city kids. It was in her nature to pursue a goal to be successful. She was stubborn and persistent. She would not give up until her goal was achieved. This was the nature of the little girl who would grow up to become one of China's most popular writers.

This piece is a compilation of excerpts taken from Sheng Ming De Na Han (生命的呐喊), *an autobiography by Zhang Yawen, a contemporary Chinese writer. The autobiography was published in Chinese by Xinhua Publishing House in 2007. "Dog Girl" tells the story of the author's childhood and her dog companion, Big Yellow.*

It happened at the beginning of the winter vacation.

One evening, the little girl came back from sledding along the river. When she went into the house, she saw a puppy lying on the *kang*, shivering. She turned to her parents and asked, "Where did you get it?"

"Your dad got it from town. Since you ran into a terrible man with a dog-fur hat, your dad said that he would get a dog for you to be your protector."

"When will this puppy be big enough to protect me?" the girl asked curiously.

"In a few months, it will grow into a big dog," said Yawen's father.

Yawen's father was right. The dog grew fast. As it had yellow fur, she called it Big Yellow. Big Yellow soon became the little girl's closest friend. He followed her like a shadow everywhere. In the daytime, he played with her outdoors and at night he slept on the floor beside the *kang*.

The day after winter vacation ended she took Big Yellow to school. They had a good time on their way, cheerfully chasing each other. Now that she had the dog, she was not afraid of wolves anymore. Whenever Big

Yellow heard a noise, he would bark loudly, his hair bristling. The wolves must have been scared away by his barking, thought the girl. When she and the dog came into the one-room school, she saw that Teacher Luo was busy surrounded by her classmates, enthusiastically talking about something. Out of curiosity, the girl approached them. She could see on the teacher's desk a couple of pencils and a metal pencil box with the characters "Labor is an honor" on it.

"Those are for you, Zhang Yawen. They are an award from Teacher Luo," one of the classmates said.

Surprised, little Yawen said, "Are they *all* for me?"

On hearing this, the classmates gave her a strange look. The eldest student, who was also the class monitor, looked angry. He had the most authority among the students and would command the class in a loud voice, saying, "STAAAND UP" as was customary whenever the teacher entered the classroom. His look made little Yawen nervous. She quickly left the teacher's desk and went to her own seat. Big Yellow followed her and lay down by her. Her classmates were still looking at the pencils and the pencil box on the teacher's desk. They did not notice that Big Yellow was with Yawen.

Before class started, Teacher Luo held up the pencil box in his hand in front of the students and said, "New Term's begun. I've bought some prizes for hard-working students of last term. Now you must choose the best student!" He glanced at little Yawen from out of the corner of his eye.

It was true that Yawen was the most hard-working and the top student in this one-room school. Last term while she was still in Grade One, Teacher Luo tested her on arithmetic, and decided to move her to Grade Three. Now with all her exam papers in his hand, the teacher said to the class, "All of you should learn from Zhang Yawen. Her home is the farthest from school, but she studies the hardest and she is the best student."

Yawen's classmates turned their heads to her and found Big Yellow sprawling near her desk. "How could she bring her dog to the classroom?" one student said loudly. "If we learn from Zhang Yawen, we all should bring dogs to school."

Teacher Luo looked at the student sternly. And the class became quiet. When he asked the students to raise their hands in approval of his choice, only one student raised her hand. Little Yawen's face turned red; she bit her lips so that she wouldn't cry in front of the class. In the end, the class monitor got the prize and Yawen didn't even get a pencil.

Little Yawen was disappointed. On her way back home, Big Yellow followed closely with his tail and ears down. The moment Yawen got home, she tearfully told her mother about the unfair award, "Why didn't my classmates choose me even though I was the top student? I really loved that pencil box and I thought that pencil box should be awarded to me."

Yawen's mother didn't answer. In the dim light of a kerosene lamp, she was stitching a sole to make a new pair of shoes for the little girl. Then she said casually, "Yawen, I came from a rich family. But I never asked for anything from my father, no matter how poor I am now. The day I got married, my father told me not to come back home to sponge off him, no matter whether I was rich or poor."

Yawen didn't understand why her mother said this to her. Her story had nothing to do with what happened to Yawen that day. But she would never forget what her mother said afterwards, "You must remember in your heart never to be greedy, not even for small gains, whether you are poor or rich. Instead, you must live with a big ambition."

Yawen's father also cut in, "No big deal; it's only a pencil box. The old saying is, 'Don't eat food handed out in contempt.'"

Little Yawen was too young to understand this saying by her father, and she had no clue what "greedy for small gains" meant, but she remembered what her parents said.

Not long after, to her surprise her father bought her a pencil box exactly like the one offered as the prize. Yawen was overjoyed. Next day, with Big Yellow accompanying her, she took it to school. A couple of boys saw her new pencil box and started teasing her, "Zhang Yawen, our teacher bought you the pencil box secretly, right?"

"No, my dad bought it for me," she insisted.

"No! Teacher Luo bought it for you! You're his favourite because you kiss his ass," yelled a big boy.

Kicking up the dirt around her, he grabbed the pencil box away from her, and passed it around to the other boys. Seeing this, Big Yellow ran at the boys, barking loudly enough to scare them away. They dropped the pencil box on the ground. Big Yellow picked it up and ran back to little Yawen.

The pencil box was full of dirt. Yawen dusted it off and saw some scratches. With tears in her eyes, she went to Teacher Luo and reported the incident. He rebuked the boys and also warned the big one, "If you act up again, I'll fix you."

After school, Big Yellow and Yawen walked home. Not far from the school, the boys caught up with her, led by the big boy. Instinctively, she put her right hand on her school bag, feeling for the pencil box. Two boys ran ahead, and Big Yellow chased them, barking. Then the big boy snatched the school bag and took out the pencil box. He threw it onto the ground and stepped on it. By the time Big Yellow ran back to charge at him, he ran away saying, "If you tell the teacher on me again, I'll push you into the river and you'll drown there."

Big Yellow chased after him.

"Come back, Big Yellow," Yawen shouted through her tears. The dog turned around and picked up the broken pencil box in his mouth, and gave it back to Yawen. She took the pencil box home and pleaded with her parents to send her to another school, the one that was in town. Her father said, "It will take you two hours to walk to that school."

"I'm afraid of those boys. But I'm not afraid of the distance. Those boys will bully me without end. Worse than that, they will kill Big Yellow sooner or later."

After two days, Yawen spoke to Teacher Luo, "I want to transfer to the school in town."

"Why do you want to change schools?"

She lowered her head, looking at her toes without saying anything.

When Yawen was leaving the school that day, all the students came out to see her off and bid her farewell. Those boys came out too, seemingly embarrassed but also looking triumphant.

Teacher Luo walked with Yawen to the riverside. He took out two pencils, exactly the same as the ones given for the prize. He handed them to her, "Yawen, I hate to see you go. You are the most intelligent student. But it might be good for you. The school in town is more like a school and much better than here. I can tell that you will study well in whatever school you go to. When you make great achievements in the future don't forget to come back to see Teacher Luo wearing a worn-out jacket with many patches on it," he said with a melancholy smile.

This was the last time Yawen saw Teacher Luo. Later she learned that he killed himself on the railway track. When she heard the sad news, she cried. The image of Teacher Luo on her first day of school returned to Yawen — a barefoot skinny man wearing a worn-out padded jacket with a straw rope around his waist.

Nancha County Primary School was at the northern foot of a mountain. To go to school every day, Yawen had to cross Yongcui River and walk through the county seat, thus having longer walk to school. It was more than 30 *li* round trip. But the school was much better; at least it had a playground fenced by mud walls and a brick classroom building. Cheerfully, Yawen walked towards the school gate with Big Yellow. To her surprise, a wiry old man stopped them at the gate and hoarsely said, "Stop! Which class are you in?"

"I've just transferred here and don't have a class yet."

"What?" Looking at the dog, he said, "You know you can't bring a dog to school."

"Yes……"

"Then why have you brought the dog here? You can't do that," he yelled.

"Today is my first day and I promise that I won't bring the dog tomorrow. Please let us in!"

"No, you can't take the dog in with you no matter what."

Yawen looked for a spot where she could leave Big Yellow for the day. She took him to a sheltered spot outside the mud wall around the school and told the dog, "Sit and stay!"

While Yawen was in class, Big Yellow stayed outside the school gate. When the bell rang at the end of class, Yawen rushed out of the gate and Big Yellow was there. He jumped up and down, waving his tail. Yawen's classmates saw her with Big Yellow and said to her, "Hey, dog girl, see you tomorrow."

Yawen and Big Yellow went to school together every day after that. The dog seemed to understand the routine. On their way to school, he followed his young mistress without any distractions. Once school was over, it was their fun time. They chased each other, frolicking on the hilly road. Yawen picked wild flowers along the way and made a wreath to put on her head. She also put one around Big Yellow's neck. Whenever Yawen's mother saw the little girl and Big Yellow running back home with their wreaths, she would say to herself, "This girl is still too young to know sorrow!"

Her father sadly nodded in agreement.

One rainy morning Yawen and Big Yellow had to take a ferry to cross the river. Unfortunately, the ferry man stopped his service that day because there were few passengers. Yawen went into the ferryman's shed and saw him in his straw rain cape, smoking a long- stemmed pipe . The shed smelled of tobacco. The smell was so strong that Yawen felt her throat tightening and eyes burning. "Uncle, could you take me and my dog to the other side of the river? We have to go to school," she pleaded.

No matter how hard Yawen begged the ferryman, he didn't budge. So she and Big Yellow walked beside the river for almost an hour in the rain. Big Yellow's ears drooped and he looked smaller with his damp fur close to his skin. But he followed Yawen closely. When they got to school, it was almost the end of the first class. Like a drowned rat, Yawen stood at the door barefooted. Seeing the rain water still running down from her hair and face, her classmates started hissing, "Hey, dog girl, now you are a drowned cat!"

Teacher Liu, who was writing on the blackboard, looked at her and said nothing. Shyly and awkwardly, she waited for the teacher's permission to let her go to her seat, Yawen stood by the door with water running down from her body to the floor. He ignored her until the bell rang, and turned to Yawen angrily, "Do you know what kind of students I dislike most?"

Yawen was still standing at the door and lowered her head, shivering and daring not to look at him.

He went to Yawen and raised her chin, saying sharply, "I'll tell you, I hate to see students late for class."

Still with her eyes lowered, she said in a faltering voice, "Teacher, I'll never be late again."

"Will you remember what you said?" the teacher sternly asked.

"Yes, I will."

At this moment, Teacher Zhao, her homeroom teacher, came into the classroom. Without a word, she pulled Yawen out of the classroom and took her to the teachers' dorm. Taking a shirt from the cabinet drawer, Teacher Zhao asked Yawen to take off her shirt and change into the one she gave to her. Teacher Liu, who had followed Teacher Zhao to her dorm, looked displeased. He was just about to say something but was stopped by Teacher Zhao, "This student lives in the mountain village south of No. 8 Bridge. She has to walk more than ten *li* on hilly roads to school. She takes a dog with her in case of wolves."

Teacher Liu looked at Yawen with surprise.

Yawen won honors for her mid-term exams, and Big Yellow gained status as well. Teacher Zhao asked her to come to the front of the class. With her hand on Yawen's shoulder, she said to the whole class, "From now on, don't call Zhang Yawen 'the dog girl.' You should all learn from her, the diligent girl."

From that day on, no one called Yawen 'dog girl' anymore. Her classmates even helped to set up a doghouse. Big Yellow would never be bothered by wind and rain again.

After school one day, Yawen was just about to run out of the classroom when Teacher Zhao stopped her, "Wait for a moment, Zhang Yawen. Teacher Liu and I are going with you to visit your home."

"Really? That's exciting!" The girl was so happy that she jumped up and down. No teacher had ever visited her humble home!

In the beautiful hour at dusk, Teachers Zhao and Liu, and Yawen walked towards her home with the red sky tinted by the glow of the sunset. All the way, Yawen was as happy as a bird, singing and laughing. Big Yellow was happy too, running in front and at the back of the walking threesome. From behind them, Yawen watched Teacher Zhao's two long braids while she and Teacher Liu walked together, following Big Yellow in the lead. The braids were pitch black and swung to and fro when she walked.

Yawen had short hair. Mum said long hair attracted lice, she told herself. She loved Teacher Zhao's long hair. Imitating Teacher Zhao's walking style, she thought to herself, "I'm going to use corn tassels to braid my hair like Teacher Zhao's." Imagining herself walking with her two long braided plaits swinging to and fro, Yawen felt so excited that she suddenly said loudly, "Teacher Zhao, your plaits are pretty!"

Hearing this, both teachers looked back; Teacher Zhao glanced at Teacher Liu with a smile.

In a mysterious way Teacher Liu asked, "Zhang Yawen, do you know what the relationship between Teacher Zhao and me is?"

Shyly, she shook her head.

Teacher Liu patted Yawen's head, "What an innocent girl you are!"

Yawen looked at her teachers, puzzled.

When they got to the river bank, the two teachers decided to take the ferry to cross the Youngcui River. After crossing the river, they walked along the hilly road for quite a long distance. When they came to the wet marshland, Yawen walked at the front as a guide and asked

Big Yellow to walk behind. In the marshland were logs here and there. Yawen used them as a footbridge. She jumped from one log to another. Some of the logs were not easily seen. She kept looking back and telling her teachers to follow her steps in case they fell into the water. Even so, very soon their shoes and socks were thoroughly wet.

Teacher Zhao asked Yawen, "How can you go to school with wet shoes and socks every day?"

"I carry a pair of dry shoes in my bag and change them at school."

Teacher Liu said, "You're a tough little girl. Why do you go to a school so far from your home?"

"I want to find a job in the city when I grow up," answered Yawen with a smile.

"What are you going to do when you grow up?" Teacher Liu said, imitating Yawen's childish tone.

"Sing!" Yawen replied instinctively, "I love singing and I want to be a singer on the stage."

"Have you ever *seen* a singer on the stage?" Teacher Liu asked.

"No, but I saw a lot of circus performances on the street. People put coins in the basket for the performance."

"Why do you like singing?" Teacher Liu continued.

"I want to sing for my dad and mum."

Having heard Yawen say that, they both laughed, sending Teacher Zhao falling into the water. Teacher Liu helped her out. Big Yellow barked.

"Remember Zhang Yawen. If you want to become a singer, you sing not just for your parents but for the vast masses and yourself," Teacher Liu corrected her with a smile.

After crossing the marshland and turning at the mountain pass, they saw a few houses in the village. It was late sunset; smoke was curling upward from the kitchen chimneys. They heard a few barks.

Teacher Zhao asked Yawen, "Which house is your home?"

She said with a smile, "Guess!"

Pointing at a thatched hut at the village entrance, Teacher Zhao asked, "Is that your home?"

"Nope!"

She pointed at another thatched hut, and Yawen said, "That's not it either! Well, let me tell you. The most run-down, smallest hut is my home!"

Teacher Zhao looked at her, doubtful. From very far, Yawen spotted her mother squatting at the door burning mugwort to keep mosquitoes out of the house. Every night, her mother would do this; otherwise the mosquitoes were so numerous that they couldn't go to sleep. From a distance, Yawen shouted, "Mum, my teachers are here."

At the sound of her voice, Yawen's mother straightened her back, and stood up in shock; she was wearing a pair of leggings and a *dajin* blouse. She pushed her hair back close to the bun at the back of her head just above her neck. Then she raised the edge of her blouse to dry her tears caused by the smoke. She looked at her faraway daughter standing with the two teachers.

When they came closer to the house, Teacher Zhao asked Yawen doubtfully, "Is that your grandma?"

"No, that is my mum," she corrected.

At this moment, Yawen's father came back from the field, holding a hoe. Immediately recognizing the two adults as his daughter's teachers, he stepped on the burning mugwort and said in embarrassment, "Excuse the mess. My humble house is in shambles. Since you are here, please have a simple meal at our place if you don't mind. I'll be back soon." Saying this, he turned round. Yawen understood immediately that Dad would go to the neighbor's to borrow some flour. Teacher Zhao stopped him, "We're not going to have a meal here. We're here just for a quick visit."

Holding Teacher Zhao's hand, Yawen pleaded, "Teacher, please have dinner with us. My mum's dumpling soup is very delicious!"

"It's going to be dark soon. Next time, we'll stay for dinner," Teacher Zhao said gently, patting Yawen's head.

Then the teachers looked at the low smoky dark hut and went inside. In one corner there was the stove with a black empty pot on it. Most of the floor space was taken by the *kang*, on which there was a small and low table. The walls were plastered with newspapers. Teacher Zhao looked at the newspapers closely and couldn't tell what was printed on them. She couldn't tell whether it was because of the smoke from the burning mugwort or if the newspapers had been already darkened by smoke from another time. While she was glancing around the room, she took a handkerchief from her pocket to wipe her eyes. Teacher Liu stood behind her, looking around the room. Thinking their watery eyes were caused by the smoke, Yawen said, "Teacher Zhao and Teacher Liu, come to the yard and sit outside."

Yawen's parents were cleaning the yard while Yawen and her teachers came out. Seeing the teachers out into the yards, Yawen's father moved away from the burned mugwort. Her mother used her blouse sleeves and her hands to clean the flat surface of the piers, and said to Yawen, "Ask your teachers to sit on the *muduns*."

Teachers Liu and Zhao sat on the *muduns* facing the shed door and Yawen's parents squatted in the doorway. Yawen looked at the teachers and her parents cheerfully while they talked.

When the teachers were about to leave, Yawen's father offered to see them off to the foot of the mountains. Yawen and Big Yellow went along with them. At the entrance to the mountain pass, her father said to the teachers, "Go through the pass and take the ferry. Otherwise it will be dark before you get back to the town."

Grabbing the hand of Yawen's father, Teacher Liu said seriously, "Uncle, you have a wonderful daughter. She will certainly amount to something."

That night Yawen was so excited that she couldn't go to sleep. While swatting mosquitoes, she heard her parents talking with sighs, "Alas, what a pity! The teachers treated our daughter so well but we couldn't even make them stay for a meal."

"What could we give them in return? We don't even have flour at home. Well, someday we'll try to reward them for taking care of our daughter." From then on the two teachers treated Yawen even better.

One day when school was over, it was dark with thunder and lightning, and rain began pouring down violently. All the classmates ran home except Yawen. She was standing by the door in the hallway, watching outside worriedly. Teacher Zhao saw her, "The rain is too heavy. Stay here today with me in the dorm."

"How is it possible?" She felt overwhelmed by this special favor.

"Why not? I live by myself in the dorm."

"But I have Big Yellow waiting for me in the shed outside the mud wall."

"We can feed him later when the rain stops and he can stay in the shed overnight." suggested Teacher Zhao. Then she took Yawen to the dining hall and they had a good meal of rice, which Yawen could only have for the Festival dinner. In the evening, Yawen didn't want to sleep on Teacher Zhao's bed, insisting instead on sleeping on a long chair.

"Why don't you sleep on my bed? This bed is big enough for both of us," said Teacher Zhao.

Lowering her head, Yawen said in a low voice, "I'm afraid that the lice in my clothes will……"

"What? I had lice when I was young. It's natural for kids to have lice."

"My Mum said lice like us because we sweat a lot and we don't have enough clothes."

"That's okay with me. I can share your lice so that they won't suck your blood," Teacher Zhao said with a smile.

Little Yawen didn't understand humor at all. "Teacher Zhao, you are so nice to me."

That night Yawen shared a quilt with Teacher Zhao. She had never slept in a bed like this; she had never been so close to city people. She felt the soft and smooth sheet, smelled the fragrance of her teacher's hair. Listening to the thunder and splashes of rain, she stayed awake for a long time, thinking of her parents who might also be awake because they didn't know where their daughter was in such a heavy storm.

Winter vacation was coming. Yawen took Big Yellow to school to get information about her homework. Through the keyhole of the classroom door, she saw Teacher Liu playing the accordion and Teacher Zhao singing. When she noticed Yawen, Teacher Zhao asked her in to sing a song for them. Without hesitation Yawen started singing loudly, "Big and red flowers are everywhere, and little friends are playing here……"

After her singing, Teacher Liu said, "Hey, that's really good. Your singing is sweet, clear, and melodious."

Surprised, she asked Teacher Liu, "How come you're a math teacher, but you can play the accordion?"

"Why can't a math teacher play the accordion? If you'd like to, I can teach you how to play it, too." Teacher Liu said with a smile.

"Really!?"

"Of course!"

But Teacher Zhao looked at him, and then she turned to Yawen, "Zhang Yawen, tell me the truth, are we good teachers?"

"Yes, you're both good teachers."

"Would you miss us if we leave here?"

"Of course, I'll miss you." She thought that they were just leaving for winter vacation.

Touching Yawen's head, Teacher Zhao said to her, "Remember that you must work hard and study well and then you'll be very promising."

"Yes, I will." She thought they wanted her to review and remember what she had learned that term.

Yawen spent her winter vacation in anticipation: she wanted the new term to start sooner so that she could learn how to play the accordion with Teacher Liu.

On the first day of the new term, with a bag of pine nuts her mother had fried, Yawen went to school full of good cheer. She went to the teachers' office, looked through the keyhole of the door to find no teachers. She asked a woman teacher about Teacher Zhao. She told Yawen "Teacher Zhao won't come back because she's gone home for her wedding with Teacher Liu."

Yawen was surprised to hear the news, and then she asked eagerly, "Will they come back after the wedding?"

"No, they've got jobs in their hometown."

What a shock to Yawen. On her way home, she cried and Big Yellow followed her closely with his tail down.

One horrible thing happened to Little Yawen that year.

Yawen's father said that the river ice was starting to melt and for three days he didn't allow Yawen to go to school. On the fourth day, Yawen pouted and then yelled at her father, "For days you said the river ice is melting. But it hasn't melted yet. I want to go to school today."

"The river ice in early spring is not reliable. It can break easily."

"The ice in the river is thick and I'm small and light. It won't break."

"You little brat, you never understand your parents," her father scolded, and then went to the pigsty behind the shed.

Yawen seized the chance to run out with her school bag. Big Yellow followed her and they came to the river. She saw that it was still covered in ice and snow. Stepping on the ice, she heard cracking sounds but the ice did not break. She started complaining about her father, "Dad told lies. It's not the time for the river to break up yet."

In the evening on her way back from school, to her surprise Yawen saw floes running along the river, large white ice blocks crowded together like a flock of white sheep. Being silly, she wasn't afraid at all; instead she enjoyed watching the floes floating. When she found a big moving ice block, she jumped to it, jumping from one block to another. Big Yellow followed her but the two never stood on the same ice block. When there was a large gap, she had to jump hard before the ice block sank, and then she would hurriedly move to another. Her shoes got soaked very soon and she felt her feet becoming icy cold, which slowed her down. Big Yellow seemed to understand her situation, jumping ahead of her, turning back and waiting for Yawen to catch up. However, when they got onto the grassland and heard the withered yellow grass rustling in the early spring wind, Yawen felt something strange. Big Yellow alertly raised his ears several times and barked wildly. Somehow the rustling sound disappeared once Big Yellow barked. Yawen looked around, trying to figure out what was hidden in the grass. The more she listened, the more she felt certain that the rustling was caused by the wind. Not far from her, Yawen saw two animals moving in the grassroots. Suddenly she was terrified, feeling her scalp tightening. Instinctively, she moved her school bag to her chest, and started running. Meanwhile she found the rustling sound approaching closer and closer. She shouted at Big Yellow desperately, "Hurry, Big Yellow! Hurry!"

Big Yellow understood her desperation. Out of instinctive loyalty, he bent his body and jumped into the grass. In a wink, Big Yellow was buried in the grass. Yawen couldn't see what was happening in the grass. But hearing a wail, and then fierce sounds of biting and growling, she trembled with fear. Big Yellow's barking became lower and his painting more laborious until Yawen could not hear anything at all.

Yawen cried desperately, "Big Yellow—hurry up—"

Suddenly the marshland was quiet. Nothing could be heard except Yawen's desperate crying and shouting, "Big—Yellow—". Yawen ran home. She pleaded with her father, "Dad, something has happened to Big Yellow. Go and get him back!"

Immediately Yawen's father understood what had happened. Instead of calming Yawen down, he started yelling and scolding her, "You little brat. The starving wolves have already torn Big Yellow apart. They are the most horrible animals in spring. You're lucky. Without Big Yellow, the hungry wolves would have you as their prey. "

"Dad, I beg you to go and save Big Yellow. Maybe he's still alive," implored Yawen, crying.

Her father found a wooden club in the yard, and some matches. Taking them, he yelled at Yawen, "Come and follow me!"

When they got back to the grassland, they saw several white bones and a pile of dog fur.

Little Yawen couldn't accept the fact. She still believed that Big Yellow was alive. She followed her father closely back on their way home, shouting and crying, "Big—Yellow—." She yelled in a hoarse and feeble voice, hoping Big Yellow would appear in front of her, running, jumping and waving his tail.

That night, lying on the *kang*, Yawen couldn't sleep for weeping. Her pillow was wet with tears. Thinking of Big Yellow following her to school in past days, she regretted that she didn't command Big Yellow to stay behind her. Big Yellow suffered as much as she in the wind and rain. She couldn't imagine what her life would be without Big Yellow. How could she walk alone in the desolate grassland and cover the long and tedious mountain roads without Big Yellow as her companion?

Yawen's mother was up that night with her smoking pipe flashing in the dark shed. The shed was full of a strong tobacco smell and Yawen felt her throat burning. Her mother murmured to her husband, "If it were not for Big Yellow, our daughter would have lost her life. I'm sure that tomorrow when she walks in the marshland by herself to school, she will be scared to death. We have to stop her from going to school. If tragedy happens to her, we would be criminals."

Yawen's father kept silent, sighing and breathing hard.

Her mother said again, "Think of something that could keep our daughter safe."

"What else can we do? We can do nothing." her father cut in angrily, "It all depends on her own fate. She should stop going to school. What's the use of a girl going to school? Girls aren't up to anything great!"

Hearing this, Yawen became very angry. What was wrong with girls? Girls were human beings as well as boys. All the boys in her class didn't study as well as she did. She would never believe that boys were better than girls. She knew already that her mother had worked harder than her father, and could handle difficulties better than him. Starting very young, she had this rebellious idea—she must achieve something. Suddenly she said in a hoarse voice loud enough to be heard, "I'll go to school tomorrow. I would rather be eaten by wolves than stay at home with you."

Her parents were shocked by this sudden shouting; they looked at Yawen with eyes wide open.

In the dark, Yawen saw her mother sit up, knocking her smoking pipe on the edge of the *kang*. Her mother said to her father sharply, "I won't see my kid suffer anymore. This is not a life for human beings. If you want to stay here, fine! But I'll take her and leave this awful place!"

Little Yawen was worried about her mother. As long as she could remember, her mother was very obedient. It was her father who always got angry with her mother. She was afraid that he would beat her mother because of her rebellion. She jumped out of her quilt, and moved quickly by her mother. Side by side, they looked at the father in the dark. Surprisingly, he sat there and kept silent. Yawen didn't know if it was her mother's first time fighting against him, or her father's own guilt that made him mild and speechless.

Yawen admired her mother, who never retreated at critical moments; instead she would support her sad family with her weak body.

Early next morning, Yawen was just about to leave for school when she heard her father shouting from the *kang*, "The ice floes have not finished yet, and there won't be any ferry today."

"I'll come back if there is none," replied Yawen. She started running outside and still could hear her father, "You brat...."

Yawen's mother followed her and shouted, "Wait, I'll go with you."

"Nope!"

"You'll be scared when you reach the marshland."

Actually, that was true. Yawen WAS scared. "But I still want to go to school..." she replied to her mother.

"Wait, I will walk with you to the mountain pass."

At the mountain pass, Yawen urged her mother to go back. Patting her shoulder, her mother said, "I'll stand here and watch you go through the marshland. Be careful of the ice blocks. They are still floating. Mum will help you with the classes you miss. Come back earlier, okay?"

Yawen nodded and then went towards the marshland. She turned back at her mother, tears running down her face.

Upon entering the marshland, immediately Yawen was haunted by the horror of the day before. She seemed to hear Big Yellow barking and wolves growling in the grass. She thought "They might jump at me at any time and tear me up as they did Big Yellow. They would eat me and only leave small bones there…"

But Yawen had no choice except to go deeper and deeper into the marshland. The way through the grass seemed extremely long for her now. She was so tired that she slowed down, breathing hard. It was too quiet so she started singing. No, she was not singing but wailing to overcome the horror in her young heart.

Finally Yawen got out of the grassland. She ran to the river and found a few floating ice blocks. But even better was the sight of the old man starting up his ferry service! What good luck for Little Yawen!

Arriving at school, as if by instinct Yawen walked along the school wall to Big Yellow's shed. Suddenly she realized that Big Yellow was not with her. She ran back to the gate, tears in her eyes. During recess, she wanted to run to look at Big Yellow, then she remembered that Big Yellow was no longer there.

On her way back home in the evening, Yawen's heart trembled. But no matter how scared she was, she had to go through the grassland. Suddenly she saw a thin, tiny figure at the edge of grassland with her grey hair blown upwards by the late evening wind. That little figure was looking towards the far end, with her hands shading her eyes from the light of sunset.

"Mum—" Yawen cried out in recognition. Nothing could be happier for her than seeing her mother at this moment. Opening her arms, she ran towards her like a little swallow.

This is a compilation of excerpts translated from

张雅文：狗娃，节选、编译自《生命的呐喊》，新华出版社，2007

The Hawthorn Tree at the

Beginning of My Life

from *The Call of Life*
by Zhang Yawen, translated by Tina Sim

My mother told me that it was a late autumn dusk, cold first snowflakes drifting from the gloomy sky.

My mother, carrying a big belly, was squatting on the hillside collecting hawthorn berries when she suddenly felt something warm trickle down from her lower body. She knew that I had ruptured my water bag, and was going to be born. She felt the crown of my head, which was moist; a little exertion and I would be born there, under the hawthorn tree, amid the fallen leaves and the drifting snowflakes. She quickly untied her smock to support my head, and crawled, or rather, rolled homeward. About midway, It became too difficult to move so she inched her way forward until my father came hurrying along with our yellow dog.

Perhaps because my mother had held me too tight, or perhaps all the amniotic fluid had flowed away, even after she reached home, even though my head had already crowned, I refused to be born. My mother remained in labor till late afternoon the next day before I finally emerged into this chaotic world, and became, in an impoverished family, another hungry mouth to feed.

My arrival not only increased the burden of a family that already numbered over 10 but also embarrassed my 43-year-old mother so that she didn't want to meet other people.

At that time, my brother's wife, having just given birth to my niece, was pregnant with a second child. In those years, for a mother-in-law and daughter-in-law to be with child at the same time was a shameful matter. My mother did not want to walk around the house with her large belly, so she would leave early every morning to work outdoors — shelling peas, husking corn, collecting haw berries —and return home after it got dark.

The minute I was born, my mother tucked me away in

the cupboard under the *kang*.

During her confinement month, my mother did not even have an egg to eat. She ate sorghum like the rest of the family and by the third day after my birth was back at work on the farm. My mother was getting on in years and did not have nourishing food to eat, so she did not have enough milk. I was so hungry I cried constantly. My mother took sorghum grains that were half-cooked, ground them with her teeth mouthful by mouthful, spitting each mouthful out into a piece of cloth, and then squeezed out the sorghum liquid for me to drink. People called this piece of cloth "a milking pad." Perhaps it was this grinding of the tough sorghum grains during the confinement month that caused her to lose all her teeth before she turned fifty.

My mother said, "Back then, children were like livestock and there was no such thing as milk powder. While there was not enough milk, the 'milking pad' served as a substitute. If the child was blessed, he lived; if he was unlucky, he died."

As a woman my mother went through a lot of hardships. She gave birth to seven children, two of whom died young; and except for my elder brother, she herself cut the umbilical cord for the rest of the six of us. During that era, the entire country was mired in poverty and struggled to make a living. Women, who formed the lowest strata of society, eked out an even more miserable existence.

Actually, my mother had been born into a rich family with good educations. Her family was famous in Mazhai for being the richest around and owned over 40 *shang* of arable land. When she was 16, she became blind in one eye, and, at 23, was married to a man younger than her by six years, my father, a widower. My mother was not good-looking, slight of build, and weighed just over 80 *jin*. From being the daughter of a rich man, she became, after marrying my father, a very capable farmer's wife who took care of matters on the farm and within the house too. In order to inherit the estate of a clansman who was also a Taoist master, our entire family moved to a valley, where we were the only family around; but not long after, the Taoist master demanded that my father take his daughter, born out of wedlock, as his second wife. My father refused, so the Taoist master bribed the county officials and threw my father into jail.

My mother, pregnant with her third child, took my brother and my sister along with her everywhere to seek help to get my father released, but failed.

One night, my mother, enduring labor pains, boiled up a pot of water, carried a bundle of hay into the west room, removed the mattress from the *kang* and replaced it with hay, a pair of scissors ready for use…

My six brothers and sisters were all born on hay, but I emerged from under a hawthorn tree.

My mother lay on the hay and labored until midnight before my immediate elder sister was finally born, yet with the umbilical cord twined around her neck, her body black and blue, evidently dead. My mother was very sad. She dressed the baby in a red smock and wrapped her in a bundle of hay. The next morning, she instructed my brother to throw the bundle into the back hills.

Even though her confinement was not over, my mother took my brother and sister with her to Kaiyuan County. She had through a cousin, finally tracked down the county judge handling my father's case--a dark and skinny old man named Shi. My mother told county judge Shi that my father was innocent and had been framed by the Taoist master. She begged the judge to release my father, and placed 300 silver dollars on his table. The judge uttered one sentence, "Go home and wait for your man."

Upon hearing those words, my mother quickly got on her knees and kowtowed to the judge.

Three days later, my father, who had been imprisoned for six months, was taken for the first time into the *yamen* for trial. But the judge's verdict became: "Zhang Guoliao, in disregard of the laws of the country, took liberties with his brother's wife on many occasions. I hereby..."

It turned out that Shi was also a Taoist and in a secret deal with Taoist Master Zhang, who had bribed him handsomely.

Just at this moment, three persons burst into the courtroom, causing the sanctimonious judge to be dumbstruck.

The intruder was my mother--covered in dust from her journey--with my sister and brother in tow. She had charged past the soldier who had tried to stop them, and not caring for her own life, had barged into the courtroom. My mother glared with her only eye at judge Shi and gave out an earth-shattering roar: "You of surname Shi, you are a corrupt and lawless official. You took my silver dollars yet you still find my husband guilty! I tell you, if I cannot win this case in this world of the living, I will pursue this matter in the nether world!" Upon which, in front of Judge Shi, who held the power of life and death, she shoved the wad of opium she had been clutching in her fist into her mouth.

This terrified Judge Shi, who was so afraid that my mother would die that he quickly adjourned his court.

It turned out the day after we reached home my mother had received a message from her cousin that my father's case would be heard in court the next day, and it was likely to be bad news. My mother had no choice but to hire a horse carriage to drive her through the night back to Kaiyuan.

Despite swallowing the opium, my mother did not die; she soon excreted it out. It turned out the opium had been wrapped in a layer of waxed paper. My mother's daring act shook up the *yamen*, and caused a stir in Kaiyuan County. The story of my mother risking her life to save my father was told and retold in our region for a long time.

As I write this manuscript and start to reflect on the

story of the older generation, I am deeply moved: My parents commend nothing to be proud of on the part of their children as ordinary peasants who, after moving into the city, were at the bottom of society; yet back then in the dark, carnivorous society, for the sake of their family, and to safeguard their dignity and rights, in front of the county judge who held the power of life and death, and in the face of the powerful patriarchal system, they showed no fear and for once lived like human beings, staging a tragic but inspiring scene that was sufficient to make us later generations proud. I admired my mother's courage in looking death in the eye, and my father's indomitable spirit in choosing prison instead of submission. In them I see an image of mine and the genes that have grown into my character.

This prolonged court case was finally settled.

Not long after my father came home, another major event happened. Late one night, intruders bearing guns came into our house, claiming they had lost their way, and asked my father to accompany them to Jinzhai. Jinzhai was over 20 *li* away. My father knew if he left with them, he might never return, but did not dare not go.

My mother waited till sunset the next day and still there was no sign of my father. It was not till early spring that we finally received a message from him that he had been forcibly conscripted.

The winter of the following year, my father returned, in full military attire.

My father had been forced to join Zhang Zuolin's army. The supervising officer, knowing that he was educated, assigned him to assist a senior officer with dictation and copying. Upon finding out that the Taoist master had died, my father had taken leave to come back to manage the funeral affairs, and did not return again.

After that, my father brought all of us, young and old, to this valley, where we were the only household, living a life of poverty and isolation. Led by my parents, the whole family, young and old, toiled from dawn till after dark, and yet we were still unable to fill our stomachs. My father constantly wore a frown on his face and when angered, would go outside the mountain to gamble, often for several days at one go.

Once my father did not return after three days and three nights. On the fourth night, my mother carried a large iron rod with her to look for him. Even when she was a long way off, I could hear the clang, clang, clang of the iron rod.

In the middle of the night, I was suddenly woken by a loud thwack, thwack, thwack I opened my eyes to see my dad pressing my mother to the ground and beating her with a feather duster. My second and third sisters were kneeling by my mother's side, crying. It turned out my mother had overturned his gambling table.

I quickly jumped onto the floor and knelt with my sisters. We three sisters knelt there, ramrod straight, begging our father to stop beating our mother or to beat us instead! I clung on to my father's leg and pleaded, "My good father, please stop beating mum. Please beat me instead!"

My father raised the feather duster and was really going to beat me but found himself unable to lay his hand on the naked little thing. He tossed the feather duster aside and walked out.

My mother, her body whipped into a mesh of lashes, instead of crying, quickly said to us, "Go and see if your father is leaving again. Hurry! Go and drag him back!"

The three of us hurried down to the stream and saw our father lying on a big rock, sighing away. We spent a long time persuading him before we were finally able to bring him home with us.

The next day, my mother got up early to light the fire and cook the morning meal, as if nothing had happened.

We were about to sit down to eat the morning meal when my second sister reported seeing three men coming down the hill. Hearing of it, my mother quickly helped my father to escape through the back window. It turned out that my father had lost so heavily playing cards that we would not be able to pay off his debts even if we sold everything we owned.

The three men demanded money from my mother the minute they entered the house. When my mother said she did not have any money, the three men ran to the shed where we kept our cow...

This was the first time I saw my mother flying into a rage. A tiny, skinny figure standing arms akimbo at the cow shed entrance, she shouted, "I dare you to take my cow! Yaqin, Yayan, Yawen, Shu E, Dan Sheng, all of you, come over here!" My eldest sister having been married off, my elder brother and sister-in-law gone visiting a relative, only a bunch of kids were staying at home.

Hearing my mother's call, we quickly rushed to her side and, like her , stood neatly in a row like a line of soldiers protecting our cow shed and our homestead!

Seeing that, the three debt collectors looked at each other, hesitating whether or not to break into the cowshed until finally they decided to quit, saying, "Life for life, money for debt." Then they left resentfully.

After they left, my mother said to me, "Go to the back of the hill and ask your father to come home for his meal."

I went up the hill to look for my father and found his face in tears.

From then on, my father never gambled again. That autumn he sold the entire year's harvest of soybeans to barely pay off the gambling debt.

In my memories of my younger days, my father was very irritable. Whenever he went berserk, all of us, adults and children, would be so frightened we would hide as far away from him as possible.

When he was done venting his anger, my father would run off to the stream at the foot of the mountain. He would sit there all night long and the next morning; we often found him fast sleep on a big rock. Later on, whenever he lost his temper, my mother would ask me to follow him secretly, to keep an eye on him and to ensure he did not fall asleep on the rocks lest he caught a cold and fell ill. I would quietly follow my father to the stream, take off my shoes and play in the water while my father sat on the rocks sighing and muttering unhappily to himself.

One evening when the weather was very hot, I noticed that my father's shirt was encrusted with salt . I bravely rolled up his trouser legs, took off his cloth shoes, and placed his feet into the water to cool. Seeing that he did not scold me, I started to scrub the dirt off from between his toes…

Over time, my father and I developed an understanding. Whenever we went to the stream, we would both take off our shoes and place our feet, one large pair and one small pair, into the water. The stream water trickling down from the mountains was refreshingly cool and soothed our feet.

That period of time is something I will never forget.

When night approached, in the blue blue sky

sometimes hung a full moon and sometimes a crescent moon, amid the silent tall hills around, everything quiet, no wolf howling, no humans speaking, just the stream murmuring and the toads croaking. I would sit with my father on a large rock, watching the moon being shaken into pieces by the flowing water, listening to him sigh as if suffocated by the weight of the big mountain and could barely breathe, and hearing him say things I would never know or understand…

"Hey old boy," said he—he had always called me old boy. "Your father was not meant to spend his life wielding a hoe! Your father is doing all this for this damned family, this damned family has ruined your father's life!"

These words were obviously too difficult for a child of four or five to understand. All I cared about was that in the water I used my pair of small feet to play with my father's large pair of feet. I often saw my father take from his shirt something that never left his side, a pocket watch. He would open its lid and look at it for a long time…

I felt this watch was full of mystery and wanted to touch it but my father would never let me. Once, when he had opened it, I craned my neck to have a look, and finally was able to see that it was an old watch. The silver plating on its lid had worn away to reveal its copper base. The watch case had the motif of a set of overlapping guns, and on its dial were roman numerals, just like the ones on the clock at home. As I was just reaching out to touch it, click, my father closed it. He lay on the rock, his eyes staring blankly at the starlit sky, not saying anything.

Once, when I was in the water trying to catch fish, I noticed my father looking intently at a photo. I crept over quietly to look, and saw the photo of a young, beautiful, curly-haired lady. Unable to hold back my curiosity, I asked, "Father, who is she? How come I have never met her?"

"Even if I told you who she was, you wouldn't understand!" My father quickly put the photo away, then warned, "Don't tell anyone! And don't tell you mother!"

I understood, in a confused manner, that my father's relationship with this woman was not an ordinary one.

Sometimes my father would recite from the Phoenix Hairpin poem of Lu You:

"Soft rosy hands,

wine sealed with yellow twine,

the city alive with the colors of spring,

willows covering the palace walls.

The east wind cruel,

happiness ephemeral,

a cup of sorrow, years apart.

Wrong wrong wrong!

Wrong wrong wrong!"

I asked, "Father, what are you mumbling about. Wrong, wrong, wrong, who is wrong?"

Ignoring my question, my father would continue to mutter to himself. The thing he said most frequently was a quote from Cao Xueqin's *Dreams of the Red Chamber*. "Our lives are, as Cao Xueqin says," he would say, "'a manuscript full of nonsense penned with bitter tears. Let all call the author fool, for none will feel his pain.'" It was not until I grew older that I learned who Cao Xueqin was.

After my father died my mother shared the story of my father's past romance.

My father, having attended school for five years, wrote a beautiful hand and could recite many ancient poems, being a reader of many classics. As his family was poor, when he married at 15 he did not marry the choice of his heart; when he married for the second time, my mother was not the choice of his heart either. After his forced conscription into Zhang Zuolin's army, a senior officer appreciated his education and transferred him to the army headquarters to help with dictation and copying. My father was a good-looking man and the daughter of an officer fell in love with him. When my father returned, he brought with him a cushion embroidered with four Chinese characters, *ai guo nan er* — a country-loving man — and a pocket watch.

I had always thought that the men and women of my parents' generation married without love, and were not even capable of the flame of our generation,, never expecting my father to have had such a romantic love affair, one that became the heart-wrenching regret of his life. I finally understood why my father said those mysterious things in front of a young child; because he had no one else to confide in, he turned to me, a young child who could not understand. When I remember those deep sighs he used to let out, each carrying the weight of a mountain, I can imagine how much pain he was suffering in his heart.

Merely a peasant who spends his life with a face towards the soil and back toward the sky, tussling daily with clods of earth, my father nonetheless had the sensibility of a scholar or an artist. He did not accept the dictates of fate, yet he was powerless to resist them. He had a character but he was essentially soft-hearted and kind to all. I saw in him the seed of my own born kindness. He was a lowly peasant who did not have the courage to break away from the shackles of feudal morality, all he could do was spend his whole life complaining and lamenting. He spent his entire life struggling between his own ideals and the reality of existence.

My mother, when telling me this story, seemed very calm, but I could tell from her murky and lifeless eyes that her heart was filled with pain. Actually, my mother had had an even harder life, except that she buried her misery deep in her heart and did not talk about it openly. She was more able than my father to face up to reality and to endure adversity. She constantly used her skinny body to shield my father and the rest of us from the many calamities. In my mother, I saw a generation of women that feared no tyranny and heroically stood up against misfortune and in whom are found the genesis of my own character.

In the summer of 1988, my eldest sister and I returned to our hometown after decades of absence. We went to the hillside to look for the hawthorn tree without finding it. We wondered if the tree had rotten away or been cut down now that decades had passed. After all, the tree that had witnessed my birth was no longer there.

I remember that, the year I was six, right under the hawthorn tree, when I saw my mother coming down the hill with a mound of firewood on her back, bloody cuts on her face, I said to her, "Mother, when I grow up, do not marry me off to someone in the valley. I want to marry into the city, like my eldest sister!"

I was only speaking playfully, but it hurt my mother deeply. Her eyes misted over and she patted me on the shoulder, saying, "Silly child, that will depend on your fate. I never ever dreamed of marrying into this destitute valley!"

This translation is edited by Chu Dongwei and Fraser Sutherland.

Translated from

张雅文：我生命初始的那棵山楂树，选译自《生命的呐喊》《生命的呐喊》，新华出版社，2007

Electronic excerpt provided by Zhang Yawen

In Respect and Awe

-- Preface to *Playing Games with the Devil*

by Zhang Yawen, translated by Vincent Dong

Playing Games with the Devil, with Thought for the Future is a book that cost me painstaking effort. Over a period of several years, I traveled three times to Europe to conduct interviews. Since its publication in August 2015, the book has garnered wide acclaim from both experts and general readers. It has won the Original Work of Excellence Award by the China National Administration of Press, Publication, Radio, Film, and Television, an Outstanding Work Award of the Erdos Prize for Literature of *Chinese Writers* magazine, and has been reprinted in a number of newspapers and periodicals. The very first real story in this book forms the prototype of my anti-war novel *A Chinese Woman at Gestapo Gunpoint*, the English edition of which was presented as an official gift by Chinese President Xi Jinping to King Philippe of Belgium on June 24, 2015.

I remember that, in the twilight moments of his life, Danish sailor Sindberg wrote, all his life he was drifting on the oceans in the world and hanging out with the blue sea and swaying palm trees; now that his boat of life was anchored in the retirement apartment, his shining eyes were still looking into the distance and his heart was still surging with the desire to drift about in the sea.

As one with deep love for the sea, even in the twilight of his life, he was still yearning for the call of the ocean with his heart in full sail. His once strong arms were still longing for a re-match with the waves, just as pilots look forward to the blue sky and athletes to the arena.

I am not a sailor. With a dim vision, my eyes are not shining into the distance. Instead, they are shining with the aspiration for the pursuit of life, although I am way past the age when one would pursue their dreams with bursting passion. However, dreams to me are just like the sea to the sailor and the prairie to the steed. Nowadays, my boat of life is also anchored in the harbor of twilight, but my heart is still like an eagle looking to fight.

I am a writer who treats literature as life. For me, writing is out of the need for life instead of the need for a livelihood. I am full of love for literature. Once I become aware of any good source material, I will go and conduct the interviews at any cost and with all my savings. In order to obtain source materials, I went to Russia several times on my own as one of the cross-border traders then called profiteers. I even went for interviews in war-ridden Chechen as well as countries and regions like Ukraine, South Korea, Hong Kong, and Europe.

In November 1999, intending to get source material about Qian Xiuling, I flew to Brussels all by myself with very little money in my wallet. I didn't speak the language there, and I had no money to hire a translator. Nor could I afford regular hotels or decent meals. With a bunch of Chinese-English and Chinese-French paper slips, I stayed with overseas Chinese and at temporary residences with just a quilt, without heating or even mattress or pillow. Wrongs or tears were nothing compared to the opportunity to interview this Chinese woman known as the Chinese Mother of Belgium by the Belgian people. I just wanted to introduce this great Chinese woman to the world and let her humanitarianism radiate in a world fraught with slaughter and plunder.

After a lot of trouble and great pains, I walked into Qian Xiuling's residence in Brussels. When I finally saw the elderly Qian Xiuling with her elegant demeanor and kindly countenance, I couldn't help opening my arms and warmly embracing her. From the bottom of my heart, I exclaimed, "Ma'am Qian, I am so happy to meet you!"

During over half a month of interviews with Qian Xiuling, I listened with my own ears to the 88-year-old lady talk about how she saved many Belgians with the help of Nazi general Falkenhausen during World War II. Hearing these moving stories, I felt that all my efforts were worth it. After the war, she was awarded the "Hero of the State" medal by the Belgian government and called Chinese Mother by the Belgian people. I think she is not only the pride of the Belgian people, but also the pride of the Chinese people. This shows that, during World War II, the Chinese made contributions not just in the Asian theater, but also in the European theater.

At that time, I actually wanted to visit Falkenhausen's native land of Germany. However, 15 years ago, the distance between China and the rest of the world was nowhere near as close as it is today. The entry threshold to Europe was also nowhere near as low as it is today. I had no choice but to regrettably abandon the idea.

The long 15 years have washed off all luster and glamour of the world and filtered out a lot of unimportant material. However, the long-cherished wish to conduct interviews in the native land of the Nazi general Falkenhausen had always been hiding in my heart and had never receded. Moreover, along with the increase of age, such a desire became stronger and stronger.

Then in the spring of 2014, a deep voice came from afar with a powerful summons to me: Come on! Go unearth those source materials, or it will be too late. Go write about them, about those great individuals who saved many lives: Qian Xiuling, General Falkenhausen, Rabe, Sindberg, Günther, Ho Feng-Shan… Let their noble humanity wash off bestial filthiness and awaken those with a conscience.

Such a deep calling withstood my inner frailty and hesitation and instilled an irresistible vitality into my over-the-hill life. Summoned to fulfill this unfulfilled wish for many years, I was determined to re-visit Europe to conduct interviews at all costs.

Indeed, at a time when the world was stripped of servile hypocrisy by frenzied aggression and left with naked slaughter, some people appeared in front of all living creatures like giants. Without considering their own safety, they sacrificed their own lives to kindle the fire of justice and illuminate the blood-red sky. In doing so, they left mankind a precious legacy -- the glorious radiance of humanity.

This nobility is worth writing about and worth unearthing by writers.

In August 2014, I flew to Europe for the third time, for 20-plus days of interviews.

In Nassau, Germany, I met with three mayors, two former, one current. The current mayor held my hands and said, "You are the first foreign writer and journalist to conduct interviews about General Falkenhausen. We would like to extend our warm welcome to you."

I entered the former residence of the Nazi general and listened to the three mayors and their friends talk about Falkenhausen's stories, his miserable life in old age, his reflections on the war and his tough experience in prison. I further realized that the disasters to mankind brought about by the war not only affected the people of victim countries, but also aggressor countries themselves.

The stories of Qian Xiuling and General Falkenhausen glisten with the noblest character of humanity and represent the spiritual wealth of humanity. I consider myself a lucky writer to have been able to get hold of them in the vast human sea and write and present their stories to readers so that people all over the world can forever remember them.

In Heidelberg, Germany, I sat in the study of Thomas Rabe, grandson of John Rabe, listening to him talk about how his grandpa saved over 200,000 refugees in Nanjing during the Nanjing Massacre committed by Japan. I felt the nobility and greatness of humanity.

At the seaside in Denmark, I listened to Sindberg's family talk about how he saved over 10,000 Chinese refugees during the Nanjing Massacre. I saw that the good or evil of humanity was not determined by national boundary or occupation, but depended on the personal choice of an individual's life.

Inside the Chinese Embassy in Germany, I listened to Ambassador Shi Mingde talk about the situation in Germany after World War II. I realized the deep-seated reasons for the different attitudes between Germany and Japan toward their crimes.

In front of my computer, with respect and awe for the glorious deeds of human kindness, I wrote the manuscript of *Playing Games with the Devil, with Thought for the Future*, often with tears in my eyes. I was totally immersed in writing, conversing with the spirits of my protagonists, feeling the pulsation of their spirits and exploring the essence of their lives.

The exploits of the protagonists deeply touched me and encouraged me. The nobility of their selfless lifesaving acts again and again purified my soul and tested the good and evil of my human nature. Meanwhile, the demonic fascists utterly laid bare the brutal beast in them and revealed their inhuman hideousness.

I often forgot about myself in writing. This oblivion made me throw off my armor and cease constraining myself with a writer's self-discipline. Instead, I let the keyboard take its own course and wrote to my heart's content. I even applauded what I did. What was there to be afraid of? Long gone were the times when the Chinese people were spineless, cowardly, and liable to both external and internal bullying and humiliation. Be your true self!

My emotions have never been so unrestrained and forceful and my train of thought has never been so forthcoming and uncontrollable as today.

I have several times reminded myself to be rationale instead of being too emotional. Only in being rational can one be profound and objective. However, the keyboard at my fingertips often would not heed the command of my heart. When passion burned away rationalism, words were no longer words. Instead, they became numerous bludgeons striking human nerves and causing conscious or unconscious oblivion.

With detailed and valuable material, I was able to tell those rare, indeed unprecedented stories. The words I typed out of respect and awe are not just about breathtaking stories, but also contain in-depth reflections on the future of the world, the fate of mankind, and the good and evil of human nature. With a broad mind that transcends country and nation, these internationalists sacrificed themselves to kindle justice and composed for mankind masterpieces through the ages. Their nobility has left a precious spiritual legacy for mankind,-the glorious radiance of humanity that is worth remembering forever.

Translated from

张雅文：为了心中的敬畏，《与魔鬼博弈——留给未来的思考》（节选），重庆出版社，2015

Electronic text provided by Zhang Yawen

Zhang Yawen's Calling: Rising Against All Odds

-- a study of *Cry for Life*, with a poetic summary of the

author's life

by Ying Kong

Zhang Yawen's autobiography, *Cry for Life* (*Sheng Ming De Na Han* 生命的呐喊), can be found in the series, *From Inside China* (13 books in total), which was commissioned by the Chinese National Publication Foundation in 2014 to promote Chinese literature worldwide. *Cry for Life* represents the reality of Zhang's life as a girl fighting against poverty and for education; as a writer fighting for social justice and, finally, for her copyright. As the saying goes, "The pen is mightier than the sword." If Lu Xun's *Calls for Arms* (1922) was able to wake up "many people fast asleep inside … an iron house without windows, absolutely indestructible" almost a century ago[1], Zhang Yawen's *Cry for Life* has inspired and will inspire some Chinese to realize their dreams. Using

---

[1] Lu, Xun. "Preface to the First Collection of Short Stories, *Call to Arms.*" *The Columbia Anthology of Modern Chinese Literature*: 6.
  Eds. Joseph S. M. Lau & Howard Goldblatt. Columbia UP, 2007. 3-7.

her own life experience, she encourages her readers to strive for a better life by fighting against obstacles.

Cry for Life has great significance regarding the Chinese Dream. As Zhang says about her dream, "Though my path through life has been bumpy and full of hardships, I have chosen it of my own will and I have pursued my dreams… and I have no regrets."[2] Zhang Yiwu, professor from Peking University, regards Zhang's autobiography as "the presentation of the Chinese dream in the course of its development."[3] He believes that the core of the Chinese dream is to constantly go beyond oneself to reach a new space and new possibilities, which Zhang has done in her life . Bai Miao, president of Lu Xun Literature Institute, thinks that Zhang's autobiography deals with one of the major themes in today's China, i.e. the relationship between the individual and one's milieu. Zhang claims in her autobiography, "My life is like a mirror. What it reflects are not just my experiences, but the deep broad background from which I have come" (*Cry for Life* 561). If Zhang's life is a mirror of the Chinese people, her writing

---

[2] Zhang, Yanwen. *Cry for Life*. Trans. Saul Thompson. Aurora Publishing House. 2014: 561.
[3] At a seminar on *Cry for Life* held by the Chinese Writers' Association in Beijing, 2008.

about the dream forms part of the discourse of the Chinese dream .

Born into a poor family in Northeast China during the 1940s, Zhang Yawen fully understands what life means to people at the bottom of society: "In my father and mother, I saw the tragedy and helplessness which beset so many people of their generation" (*Cry for Life* 119). Education is wishful thinking for a little girl like Zhang, who lived deep in the mountains during her childhood. However, her desire to go to school was so strong that "[e]very day, little ten year old me walked the ten kilometer round trip along the shrub-covered, animal-infested mountain path ." (*Cry for Life* 171) Little Yawen fought with wild boars, wolves, and sometimes bad people in order to go to an available school. Twenty years later, with only five years of elementary school, she fought her way through all kinds of difficulties and prejudices to become a writer. As a writer, she reported on social issues in the interest of public awareness and social justice. Her non-fictional writings, *Crossing the Land of Sadness—It's Not Just for One Village or One Person* (1989) and *Lay Down Your Hunting Guns -- It's Not Just for One North East Tiger* (1990), are stories focused on Chinese environmental issues. *Gone Through the Painful Place* (2011) is about the struggles of the Party secretary of the Fool Village in leading his people to change their fate. Most of her non-fictional offerings expose human ignorance and indifference toward society. She also visited prisoners who received death sentences to write about their lives. A novella, *How Beautiful it is to Live* (1998), expresses death-row criminals' longing to continue their lives. When reportage in China was experiencing "a low ebb, since a lot of potential source materials was deemed 'sensitive'," (*Cry for Life 453*) Zhang decided to set herself free by looking for topics abroad to "break new ground" in her writing. Using her savings, she went to Russia, South Korea, and Europe despite the language and culture barriers. Exploring primary materials, she produced groundbreaking works such as *Russian Roulette* (1994), *The Chinese Doctor for the President of South Korea* (1998), and *A Chinese Woman at Gestapo Gunpoint* (2002), the last of which became a novel and a TV drama. With such achievements, Zhang could have enjoyed her reputation as a successful writer. Instead, she chose to stand up and fight for her copyright as a screenwriter of *A Chinese Woman at Gestapo Gunpoint*. The challenge to her writing life was no less severe than her battles with a harsh life during her childhood. Nonetheless, she considered her fight for the copyright not "just a victory for [herself] as an individual defending [her] rights, it was also a victory for protection of all authors and screenwriters in the country."(*Cry for Life* 559) Zhang's life story is allegorical because she thinks that "[a] person's story is just like a country."[4] Therefore, *Cry for Life* has become a persuasive autobiography for a nation which has also fought its way onto the world stage: "China had been on its knees at the feet of the rest of the world for over a hundred years, but it never got what it had hoped to see by not fighting." (*Cry for Life* 119)

Cry for Life has met with a good reception in China since the first Chinese edition in 2007; so far it is in its fourth edition. It won the 2008 Xu Chi Reportage Prize and the 2010 Lu Xun Literature Prize, both of which are top prizes in China. At the presentation of the Lu Xun Literature Prize, a comment was made on the book to the

---

[4] Zhang, Yanwen. *Cry for Life*. Aurora Publishing House. 2014: 120.

effect that Zhang's creative nonfiction goes beyond the genre limitations and reaches the same literary effects as fiction. As an English reader and life-writing scholar, I believe that *Cry for Life* not only has much to offer in our endeavor to understand human nature and to gain insight into the workings of the particular life of contemporary Chinese writers but it also contributes to autobiography as a genre.

In "What Are We Reading When We Read Autobiography," Paul John Eakin remarks, "the narrative activity in and of autobiography is an identity activity."[5] *Cry for Life* directly or indirectly tells stories about Zhang's identity as a writer in contemporary China, how and why she becomes a writer "in constant struggle against [her] fate, in constant outcry."(*Cry for Life* 561) This "fated" narrative throughout the autobiography, as John Pilling suggests, "cannot be considered 'tragic'"[6] even though tragic accidents seem to have dogged her before and after she became a writer. In the first part of her life, the author beat the odds against several threats in her life

[5] Eakin, Paul John. "What Are We Reading When We Read Autobiography." *Narrative,* Vol. 12.2 (2004)   130.
[6] "What Are We Reading When We Read Autobiography," p. 118.

before she became a writer; in the later part, she had to fight even when she was almost dying for her reputation as a writer. Seven chapters directly discuss her oeuvre, highlighting the writing process of *A Chinese Woman at Gestapo Gunpoint,* first in a TV drama series and then in a novel. On June 24, 2015, President Xi Jinping presented the English version of this book as a gift to King Philippe of Belgium.

Even though Zhang Yawen might seem to be self-pitying: "My lot is not a happy one, and so my whole life has been a bitter struggle against my wretched fate, "(*Cry for Life* 11) *Cry for Life* has turned out to be what Stephen Shapiro calls "a comic genre in that it asserts the ego's transcendence of circumstance."[7] In Zhang's case, writing autobiography first serves as catharsis from her hopeless situation in a copyright case: "I had to have an outlet, only through pouring myself into my writing could I ease the dull ache and imbalance in my heart, only through writing could I dispel the heavy thoughts that had been weighing on me for so long and release the creative passion that I had held pent up inside me for so long! So I

[7] Pilling, John. *Autobiography and Imagination: Studies in Self-Scrutiny.* Routledge & Kegan Paul, 1981: 118.

began writing, putting my whole life into words."(*Cry for Life* 553) In the process of writing, she learns "to use emotion as a tool to become closer with the world" (*Cry for Life* 446). In the end, the "words" have turned into a celebration of life: "My life is just as it always has been: full of energy and joy" (*Cry for Life* 561). As in most autobiographies, the self in *Cry for Life* is in "a transformational or metaphorical act,"[8] in which the writing self constantly catches up with her milieu.

Unconventionally, Zhang's autobiography starts with her two deathbed wills: one for her husband and one for herself. Paradoxically, the will for herself expresses a strong desire to survive, "You can't die; you must survive this great trial of life and death!" (*Cry for Life* 11). On the one hand, the will has become an alibi for the author to tell of her unhappy lot in the past and the life-and-death situation at the moment of waiting for heart surgery. Facing her heart condition, the autobiographer questions, "When exactly did my heart begin its descent to ruins?" (*Cry for Life* 11)[9] By reflecting upon her life trajectory, she comes to the conclusion that it was the "heaven-given

---

[8] Pilling, *Autobiography and Imagination: Studies in Self-Scrutiny*. 118.
[9] Ditto.

task" of writing the screenplay of *A Chinese woman at Gestapo Gunpoint* that led her to this heart surgery and lawsuits for her copyright. On the other hand, anticipating death, however, is "a strategy for overcoming it."[10] In her case, the purpose of writing her autobiography is to bring herself "balance and equanimity" (*Cry for Life* 552) since "the legal system was not capable of delivering justice" to her. Imagining her death fits Sayre's observation: "In transforming life into destiny—in resurrecting the past as necessary—the autobiographers in effect anticipate death, because they deny their continuing historical natures in order to repeat the past."[11]

Following the chapter about her anticipation of death "The Inspiration that Brings Fresh Meaning to My Life" details how she followed up a story in the paper *Global Times* of a Chinese woman named Qin Xiuling. Qin used her connection with a Nazi general to rescue more than a hundred Belgians who had been condemned to death by the Gestapo in WWII. Zhang demonstrates how she, as a biographer, writes about the life of the Chinese-Belgian

[10] Sayre, Robert F. *The Examined Self: Benjamin Franklin, Henry Adams, Henry James*. Princeton UP, 1964: 181-2
[11] Sayre, Robert F. *The Examined Self: Benjamin Franklin, Henry Adams, Henry James*. Princeton UP, 1964: 182.

hero in a TV drama, describing her interviewing in Belgium, collecting source materials, working on the manuscript. She also introduces us the complicated networking through which she found a film company to shoot this TV drama in Europe. The autobiographer is fully engaged in playing her role as a biographer. Zhang's story about her stay in Belgium touches on the idiosyncrasies of Chinese culture, the concept of "Face:"

I'm ashamed to say that I, an author of modest means, who had spent all the money I had, swanned off to Europe with stars in my eyes, and found myself confronting that most fundamental of problems in life; I was embarrassingly short of money. All the self-respect and sense of accomplishment that I had nurtured in China were laid bare, like a peeled egg sitting alone and shiny in the middle of a plane. (*Cry for Life* 23)

In spite of the losing face, Zhang enjoys her conversation with Qian Xiuling, her visits to museums and her excitement in obtaining precious photos, all of which would testify authoritatively to the truth of herself as the screen writer of *A Chinese woman at Gestapo Gunpoint*. With all the information she needs for her writing about

Qin Xiuling's life, the now-biographer believes that the "content of this true story is so profound, so rich, so full of wild plot twists and deep, strong-willed characters, it's even more soul-stirring than the original story behind the film *Schindler's List*" (*Cry for Life* 50). To her, the material she obtains is "no less of a revelation to have stumbled upon this kind of heaven-sent material than it would be for a gold prospector who chances upon a gold mine." The style of this chapter is a mixture of the autobiographical self, the self of her subject, and part of the screen play she has written. If one were to read only this chapter, one could discern the author's strong passion for her subject, admire her tactics in conducting interviews, and celebrate her efficiency in completing the screenplay. All of these attest her validity as the screenplay writer of *A Chinese woman at Gestapo Gunpoint*.

Chapters 3 and 12 are mainly about the author's copyright case, which reveals the rampant fraud in Chinese media and legal fields. The chapter, "'Black Fridays'—I Am Driven to Death's Borders" exposes "the inner workings" of the film world (*Cry for Life* 64), which Zhang believes, "has always been a place with no law, no nationality, and no morals" (*Cry for Life* 96). Although she realizes that "a screenwriter declaring war against a powerful film company is like hitting a rock with an egg," her unyielding personality empowers her to be a writer warrior in pursuing her battle for her copyright. The chapter, "Two Last Testaments, One for Myself, One for My Husband," details the difficult process o appealing a negative judicial decision against her. Zhang's husband, who worked in law for over twenty years, warned her of the difficulties, "I warn you not to pin too much hope on the law! The law is dead, but judges are very much alive…they're also bound by all kinds of personal relationships" (*Cry for Life* 98). True enough, the legal fight for her copyright lasted seven years!

Those moments in the appeal process are "the bitterest, most bereft of hope period" in Zhang's life (*Cry for Life* 508). As a writer nurtured in her own society, Zhang "refused to believe that there was nowhere in China where people speak reason" (*Cry for Life* 552). After dealing with "judges who all had different levels of competence, different backgrounds, and different webs of social connections" (*Cry for Life* 516), Zhang admits, "I mistakenly thought that a court of law is a place where you can put right the wrongs that have been done to you and seek justice." She discovered that the court of law was "just a platform for all parties to say their lies in public and to quibble over irrelevant technicalities. One side shoots arrows at the other and vice versa simultaneously, each arrow piercing your heart and further widening the already gushing wound it has made." Even though Zhang tries her best to demonstrate how her copyright was violated and how she used legal devices to protect herself, the content of these two long chapters can be overly difficult to keep the reader's interest. One element that makes the autobiographer lose grasp of her writing is the "anger" in Virginia Woolf's words: "It was the anger that had gone underground and mixed itself with all kinds of emotions. To judge from its odd effects, it was anger disguised and complex" (*Cry for Life* 583). To relieve her anger, Zhang has provided more about her emotional reaction over the copyright violation rather than the dramatic effect of the plot. Although in the case of autobiography, "telling the truth is the cardinal rule" (Eakin 21), "autobiography is so often thought of as an art of retrospect" (Eakin 148).[12] While the dates and the people involved in her legal case are important for the autobiographer to provide significant facts, the story telling is more appealing to the reader because "Autobiography in our time is increasingly understood as both an art of memory and an art of imagination" (Eakin 5-6). The complexity of her legal case draws away the reader's interests and curiosity. Reading one hundred pages in which the writer seems to lose her capacity for imagination and creativity causes the reader to become bored with unnecessary facts regarding times, venues, rumors.

Another thing that can spoil *Cry for Life* is the dozens of quotations and mottoes from popular or famous people. Zhang might have intended to use those sayings and mottoes to erase her "primary school student" identity, which "already became a tag that was firmly stuck to me, much like the 'scarlet letter' on Hester Prynne's dress. Many people viewed me through the colored lenses of these words, in the same kind of way that people view peasants sojourning in the city" (*Cry for Life* 402). As a

---

[12] Eakin, Paul John. *Fiction in Autobiography: Studies in the Art of Self-Invention.* Princeton UP, 1985.

matter of fact, the redundant quotations add nothing to her new identity as a writer except to prove that she is well read. In an autobiography, readers expect to explore self-presentation through development of the self rather than through famous writers who are not directly associated with the self being explored or discovered.

In contrast to the chapters that examine the dates, venues, and procedures of the copyright case, *Cry for Life* is true to what Pasternak wrote in saying the "greatest works of art are those of which describe their own birth" (*Cry for Life* 61). The physical birth of her life is described in her own cultural context: "At the same time I was born, my older brother's wife had just given birth to my niece … In those days, it was a matter of embarrassment for a woman to be with child at the same time as her daughter-in-law." (*Cry for Life* 122) Thus, she imagines the fetal self who seemed to understand her mother's embarrassment, "I refused to finish my birth for a long time even though my head was already out. I dragged out my entrance into the war-ruined world." Blaming herself for adding to the burdens of the already impoverished family, she feels sorry for her mother as saying "my forty-three-year old mother became shy about seeing other people." For this Zhang's parents called her "Little Miss Extra."(*Cry for Life*: 122)

Interestingly, with no Christian background, Zhang considered her survival of the heart surgery as a resurrection of Jesus Christ. This epiphany came to her while she was allowed to observing the doctor doing heart surgery because she was commissioned to write reportage about the doctor. She imagined herself as lying on the operating table suffering from the pain just as Jesus endured his torture to be reborn: "In that moment, I felt as if I had been born again, as if I had returned to my true state." (*Cry for Life*: 539) The grouchy and angry self died; a new self was born:

I gazed out of her journey of a new life. I gazed out of the window at the passing scenery; everything felt at once unfamiliar and intimate, and I had a strange, vague sense of being in some other world and an insatiable feeling that I could not see enough with my eyes…. Everything that I had taken for granted in the past suddenly seems so beautiful and dear to me. (*Cry for Life*: 538)

With this new self, the autobiographer becomes more complacent: "What about those who cannot do so, who are powerless to resist the injustice they face? What can they rely on to bring equanimity to their hearts" (*Cry for Life*: 554). Compared with those who are powerless, she becomes more graceful than ever because now she can turn her life-writing from the "venting of emotion" to a calling to "those poor young people who are still struggling to free themselves from their own hardships" (*Cry for Life*: 559). Once the motivation of life-writing turns into a driving force she no longer complains about her fate. Thus narrative tone becomes provocative: "It is not our fault that we are poor, and we can't throw away our lives for nothing just because we are poor. We must take the fight to our fates!" To this end, Zhang's autobiography is didactic and inspirational. As a matter of fact, the whole autobiography is about how the author fights through her life to gain her status as a writer warrior.

What makes Zhang a writer warrior? Zhang owes her fighting spirit to her parents: "My parents were common peasants their whole lives, remaining at the very bottom of the social hierarchy...But in the dangerous, dark, and corrupt society that China was in their day, they moved heaven and earth for the sake of their family, for its dignity and its very survival. They stood tall and fearless against a county official" (*Cry for Life*: 115). She associated the personal fate of her parents with that of her nation, "China had been on its knees at the feet of the rest of the world for over a hundred years, but it never got what it had hoped to see by not fighting" (*Cry for Life*: 119).

With her mother as a role model, Zhang acknowledged, "I admired my mother for her unwavering courage, even in the face of death, and I admire my father even more for his willingness to sit locked up in a jail rather than submit. I see my shadow cast by their bodies, and in them I can also see from what basic materials my own character was formed" (*Cry for Life*: 115). When the debt-collectors came to the door, "we lined up next to her [the mother] like a row of little soldiers, ready to protect our jail and our home" (*Cry for Life*: 136)! Little Yawen also became a warrior to protect her hunchbacked sister when she was bullied by a group of children: "I would fight with all my strength against anyone who called her a hunchback" (*Cry for Life*: 159). She fought not only with the debt collectors and the taunting boys, but also with wild animals such as wolves, wild boars, black bears, and tigers.

Ironically, the unyielding character Zhang takes from her parents also hurt them badly when she fought against their traditional ideology. At the age of 15, she escaped from home to become a skater. This was against her father's wish because in those days athletes in China were thought to have "feeble brains hidden in muscular bodies" (*Cry for Life*: 287). When she told her parents that she would marry an athlete, her father expressed his prejudice, "'Only those who had nothing else they could do in life went off to become an athlete" (*Cry for Life*: 287). Her father called athletes "eat-for-free" and he believed that "it was a waste of money for the state to cultivate athletes." In spite of her parents' opposing opinions, Zhang married the athlete.

This strong will and indomitable spirit highlights Zhang's fighting copyright infringement. She decides to fight for the common good: "I decided to continue fighting the case, not because I wanted the two hundred and fifty thousand *yuan* of my writer's fee, ... but because I demand at least some justice from the law!...I wasn't doing it any more, I was doing it on behalf of the thousands upon thousands of common people who have no backgrounds, no rights, and no influence, and to whom no doors or even windows, are open" (*Cry for Life*: 558). After seven years of court cases, Zhang won. In a more reflective tone she comments, "This wasn't just a victory for me as an individual defending my rights, it was also a victory for the rights protection of all authors and screenwriters in the country" (*Cry for Life*: 559). Zhang's narrative meets the Chinese people's psychological needs and national demands. He Xilai, a famous Chinese literary critic, remarks, "Zhang Yawen's reflection upon her sixty years of life and writing provides us with the image of a woman who is aggressive, stubborn, unyielding, and unbeatable... Her striving for a better life and her fighting spirit are the precious characteristics of a rising nation and of its intellectuals...She does not only cry for her own life in times of adversity, hardships and setbacks, but calls for arms on behalf of the diligent and strong nation." The strident calls to fight for a better life are the themes highlighted in this autobiography.

Cry for Life also provides readers with fascinating stories of cultural myths in China. The "magical power" of Master Zhang, a Daoist priest and a senior member of the author's own family clan, is a story of how Zhang's father fought against the power of the dark world controlled by the Daoist priest. The story of "Old Mrs. Fox" tells how her family is tricked by superstition. Instead of criticizing her parents' superstitious traditions, Zhang gives a reasonable explanation why "that basket and chopstick dictated almost every aspect of our lives": "Back then people were ignorant about many things. They were not able to be the masters of their own fate, so they put their fates in the hands of imaginary spirits" (*Cry for Life*: 161). The story of two men and one woman living together under the same roof harmoniously reveals a humanistic culture in rural China, where "if a man's health was bad and as a result couldn't fulfill the duties expected of him as the man of the house and as a husband, his wife could take another man if she so desired." (*Cry for Life*: 185)

Memory talk, telling stories from one's memory, is another feature in *Cry for Life*. Through memory talk, Zhang revisits her parents and sisters in the process of writing about their stories. She identifies herself with her father who fought with Master Zhang, and identifies herself with her mother who fought with the court to rescue her husband. Memory talk not only provides Zhang with the source for her life writing but also for her creative writing: the stories of a snake with magic power, of Cherry Mountain, and of a deep well have been integrated into her writing: "These ancient and mysterious stories represented my earliest cultural awakening and also provided the material for the endless daydreams. I ended up weaving these stories into my novels" (*Cry for Life*: 138). The little girl was obsessed with the harsh life on a deep and isolated mountain, but she became elevated by imaging herself in a city she had never been to. The weird, isolated, and poor people she met have become the source materials for her creative writing. One of the characters in her novel *A woman Crossing the River of Men* is based on a real story of an old man in whose house where they stayed while they were building their own hut. He lived alone because there was no other woman on the mountain. The little girl happened to see him "sobbing loudly and holding up flower-patterned women's clothes. He cried and cried and began to stuff the clothes down the front of his trousers" (*Cry for Life*: 164). The desire to walk away from the mountain and see the outside world helped her in her later writing days to create the main character, a woman "whose heart ached to leave the mountain and find love" (*Cry for Life*: 140). As Zhang tells her readers, "My childhood gave me a deep understanding of the suffering and hardships of the peasantry, which I used to create works like *A Woman Crossing the River of Men*" (*Cry for Life*: 220).

Zhang is a good story teller when looking back at her younger self. The story of Big Brown is full of joy and sorrow. Big Brown is a dog that her father got her as a companion while she had to walk more than 15 kilometers round trip to school. Readers seem to hear the 10-year-old girl singing, "One dog, one girl, playing their way joyfully down a mountain path." (*Cry for Life*: 198) They can feel the sorrow when reading about Big Brown vanishing into a clump of grass to protect the girl from wild animals: "I couldn't see what was happening, I could just hear a tearing, biting sound that was enough to make my skin crawl" (*Cry for Life*: 211-12). The story of the red silk ribbons describes her hunchback sister's repressed longing for love from a peddler who never had a chance to express his love for the sister. The red silk ribbons have become the keepsake for love and faith for her sister, who died at the age of 24: "it was as if she had placed her last hope in them. The silk was her greatest refuge of her heart's sorrows" (*Cry for Life*: 150).

As a screenwriter, Zhang is good at adopting cinematic techniques to her story telling . The imagery in *Cry for Life* produces video and audio effects. Describing her mother working in the field, she writes, "The image of her tiny frame propping up a mound of firewood has been forever carved into my memory" (*Cry for Life* 138-9) The image is so strong that the tiny body under the heavy load seems to be in front of the reader. The story of how little Yawen managed to escape a child-sex offender who offered her a ride in his horse cart on a deep winter evening is very moving. The reader is treated to a dramatic word picture: from her lucky moment of being invited onto the horse-driven cart with the "dog-fur-hatted driver," the chatting between the little happy girl and the face-covered man, one of his freezing-cold hands reaching into her jacket, her smooth chest and belly, her recalling her mother's story of a bad man "tapping children's heads with a knockout drop and taking them away to some place where no people lived and chopped them up to sell on the street as meat dumplings" (*Cry for Life* 186), to the child's shouting, "Stop! I don't want to ride in your sled anymore! I want to get off! Stop!" The driver's "wolfish glance" (*Cry for Life* 187) and "his eyelashes crusted with frost," and "the image of the meat dumplings kept flashing in and out of focus in front of my eyes," the thin little girl struggling free of the driver's grip and climbing up on the back of the sled and jumping off but her "school bag caught on a wooden stake tied on the back of the sled" (*Cry for Life* 188), "like a dead dog being dragged over the ice by the speeding sled," how she "stretched out my hands to try to free my bag" and "the strap snapped", "the sound of the horse's hooves receded into the distance and I lay like a corpse on the ice," how her "mother saw my belly covered in blood and heard my tearful account" (*Cry for Life* 189). The little warrior fought with the sex-offender in "a contempt for death and danger, and defiance of violence and force" (*Cry for Life* 192).

Cry for Life is a mirror reflecting the reality of Chinese society because the stories in this autobiography have been grounded in real people, places, and events. It is a kaleidoscope of "what really happened" in today's China from the point of view of a popular Chinese writer.

Finally, I'd like to attach my brief poetic biography of Yawen inspired by her cries for life:

Zhang Yawen, a poetic "autobiography"

Zhang Yawen is my name; I have no pen name
In China, surnames come first; we identify with
    family lines
My family name is *Zhang*: a combination of *gong*
    and *chang*
Literally it means to open a bow, a weapon used in
    ancient China
The *Zhang* clan is said to start with Zhang Hui,
    inventor of the bow
Even before I was born I was given a boy's name,
    Kuiwen
as my older brother was named *Kuiwu*

Kuiwu means being adept at the sword

Kuiwen means being good at the pen

My parents wished for sons

Sadly I was born a girl; my father named me
Yawen

Ya means elegant and refined, *wen* literary

Along the lines of my older sisters *Yazhen, Yaqin,*
and *Yayan*

Names meaning noble and literate

I must be the literary girl of my family

My father wanted us to be noble and literary to
change his fate as a peasant

He lived off the land, face in the mud, back to the
sky

Worked himself to death yet found himself
penniless

Wishful he went to town to gamble, hoping for
money to feed his family

Debt collectors came to the door threatening to
put him in jail

My mother sold everything to pay the debtors

Moved to a wretched mountain ravine and started
     a life worse than humble

No villagers nearby, nor debt collectors to fear but
     ghosts behind, around the hut

thatched with straw and stalks from sorghum and
     corn

No food for us hungry children

Father and brother went to the mountain, foraged
     for food and wood

They cultivated land to grow more food

Mother and sisters worked around the hut to
     prepare food

No schools for us noble and literary kids

My sisters talked about school

I pleaded my parents to send me to school

"No school nearby, my son," my father still
     treated me like a boy

My mother and sisters looked at the mountains
     and gazed at the world beyond

while the men climbed the mountains to cut
     firewood and find food

The desire to get down from the mountains
impressed me and became my inspiration
forty years later for my novel *A Woman Crossing
the River of Men*
But how could I become a writer in the ravine
without formal education
My siblings never went to school
but I cried, "I want to go to school!"
"Wretched child of this broken family, the adults
here don't even have food
and you still want to go to a bloody school?" my
father scolded
"Didn't you say that nothing can be more
deserving of one's time than reading books?"
"Little brat, did you really talk back to me?"
"I'll go down the mountain alone to find a
school."
"I'll break your legs if you go."
I cried myself to sleep, dreaming of being at
school, yelling and shouting, "I am at
school!"

Early next morning while still asleep my father
    woke me with an angry look, "Get up!"

My mother asked me, "Didn't you want to go to
    school?

Even in your dreams, you yelled out aloud 'I'm at
    school.'"

We left the hut in the dark, father striding ahead

I ran with my little legs to catch up with him

We walked through the mountain pass, boundless
    grass, muddy land

Finally we got to a village house, the sun well
    above our head

A barefooted man with messy hair came out to
    greet us

wearing a tattered old cotton-padded jacket, a
    grass-root belt around his waist

He was my one-classroom school teacher; I
    studied hard for a year

then moved to another school because of the big
    boys' bullying

My second school stood at the foot of another
    mountain
Fifteen kilometers round trip
My father got a dog to accompany me for the
    daily three-hour walk
Dog Girl became my nickname
I trotted to school with Big Yellow each morning
And loitered towards home with Big Yellow at my
    side

My body grew strong like an athlete
before I graduated from primary school
I was chosen at the age of fifteen by Jiamusi, the
    city with an athletic team
I was trained to be a speed skater, five years on a
    mountain ice rink
Dreaming of becoming a master, a champion

But fate played a big joke on me; I was injured
    and my dream melted away
I left the ice rink in my early twenties, retired
    from an athlete's career

As a bank clerk I was not content, I went back to
    night school

Planned to finish high school and go to university

Then the Great Cultural Revolution broke out; it
    was 1966

There was no school for anyone

From friends, I borrowed foreign literature books

Read Shakespeare, Tolstoy, and Victor Hugo…

I read them under the covers of *Selected Works of
    Mao Zedong*

Started writing reading journals and found

I loved reading and was good at writing

In 1979 my city hosted a national hockey
    competition

I was encouraged by my husband, a hockey coach

to write a short poem, *Eight Hundred Million
    Citizens Come to Fight for You*

For the first time I tasted the sweetness of
    publishing

"When you are retired, you will write," my
    husband said

I told myself, "Opportunity only favors those who
understand how to pursue it."

After a writing workshop I started my first novel
The Splashes of Life

With only five years of education I published a
novel

At the age of thirty-five I gave myself to my
writing addiction

Quickly I found my knowledge of the world too
sparse

My words were too simple, my vocabulary too
small

I threw myself into reading, burrowed deeper into
books

I wrote poems, short stories, novels, and TV series

The spring of my life finally bloomed in 1980

Left my clerk job for an editorial job

At work I edited manuscripts from others, at home
I wrote for my soul

My vision widened, my heart opened, words
gushed from my pen

Suddenly my boss mocked me

"How could a five grader become a great writer?

An editor is good enough, let go your dream to be
a writer."

I refused to listen, and went to Radio and TV
University

I wanted to become a great writer, to get rid of the
"pupil" label

Persevere perspire prosper

I became a creative writer at the cultural bureau

Swam in creative oceans with my writing passions

I took Lu Xun as my model writer

I would despise evil, oppose ugliness

Stand firm in righteousness, reveal injustices

I created a sensational hit in my city

Reported blood bank corruption in a hospital

Seeing the power of my report, the cultural bureau

commissioned me to write a positive story about a
notorious mayor

Many were desperate to curry favor with the
mayor or governor

but never had a chance; I refused

People laughed, called me an idiot

Let me be an idiot!

I laughed it off, and addicted to writing my
passions

I kept these basic principles

To write diligently

To live cleanly

To not engage in flattery

To rely on my ability

To cross whatever bridge my ability would take
me

I spent my time in labor camps and prisons

Interviewed prisoners; behind their crimes I found

shocking personal stories hidden inside their
minds

Uncovered social and family problems, produced
food for thought in our society

I looked at the dejected, despairing face of a
nineteen-year-old man

facing execution

I asked him, "Qin, what are you thinking?"

He heaved a long sigh, "What's more to think about?

The only thing on my mind is to survive."

From his innocent childhood to his criminal life, I wrote a novella

How Beautiful It Is to Live

I went into the forest, wrote a report on a case of a person in jail for 17 years

wronged by an incorrect judicial verdict

while making noise about injustices dealt to others

I launched a legal case for the copyright of my play

A Chinese Woman at Gestapo Gunpoint

a true story of a Chinese-Belgian woman, Qian Xiuling (钱秀玲)

She saved more than a hundred Belgians from the Nazis

with the help of German general Alexander von Falkenhausen

I had been twice to Belgium, interviewed Qian Xiulin, the female Schindler of China

I worked day and night, completed the TV drama
　　series

It was broadcast on CCTV

My name as a playwright was changed to that of
　　the editor of my manuscript

I fought and wrote, and seven years later, the
　　name was finally corrected

My autobiography, *Cry of Life*, tells the whole
　　story of my fight

Based on that TV drama, I produced a novel with
　　the same name

Chinese President Xi Jinping presented my book
　　to King Philippe of Belgium

Cry for Life also won the Lu Xun Literature Prize

I grew up reading translated novels from the West

*One Hundred Years of Solitude, The Sound and
　　the Fury, Catch 22, The Third Wave...*

Now my books *Cry for Life, Play Games with the
　　Devil, Lessons for the Futu*re...are translated
　　into English and other languages

They are all published under the name of Zhang
   Yawen

A Chinese woman writer who fought for justices
   with her pen

Zhang Yawen, a noble woman writer my father
   wished

I didn't let him down.

Contributors, translators, and contributing editors

Chu Dongwei, Fulbright Scholar at the Center for Translation Studies, University of Illinois at Urbana-Champaign, is Professor of Translation Studies of the School of Interpreting & Translation Studies, Guangdong University of Foreign Studies, affiliated with GDUFS Center for Translation Studies, and GDUFS Center for Foreign Literature and Culture. Chu Dongwei is a member of the Guangdong Provincial Writers Association.

Tina Sim has translated for Words Without Borders; thr Asian Shakespeare Intercultural Archive; Maths Paper Press' BooksActually Gold Standards; Singapore Press Holdings; and NUS Business School.

Vincent Dong holds a master's degree in American Literature, former lecturer of English at Nanjing University and visiting fellow at Harvard University. A freelance translator for over ten years in Vancouver, Canada.

Dr. **Ying Kong** is an assistant professor of English Literature at the University College of the North, Canada. Her major research is on Comparative Literature, Indigenous Literature and Life Writing. She is also known as a Chinese scholar. She taught Chinese Culture, Literature and Cinema for East Asian Languages and Cultures at the University of Winnipeg for ten years. In addition to academic publications, she also published short stories in English. Her short story, "Lao Yang" has been selected for the anthology of *AlliterAsian: Twenty Years of RicePaper Magazine* published in the fall of 2015 by Arsenal Pulp Press.

Zhang Yawen (1944-), winner of the Lu Xun Prize for Literature and a number of other prestigious literary awards, has been a professional skier, literary editor, and writer of novels, biographies, screenplays, and non-fiction books, well known for *The Call of Life, A Woman Crossing the River of Men, A Chinese Woman at Gestapo Gunpoint, The Russian Roulette, We Shouldn't Share the Same Sky, Mama, Give Me a Hand, Life of Ice and Snow, The Chinese Physician of the President of South Korean*, among other books and screenplays.

United States Production and Public Relations
Tao Yang, IntLingo Inc., NY

Chinese Contact and Public Relations
Jiang Sheng, Zilin Limited, Guangzhou

Subscription Information Update

Chinese Literature and Culture (ISSN 2332-4287 print; ISSN 2334-1122 online) is now discoverable in EBSCOhost research databases: the **One Belt, One Road Reference Source** collection and the **Humanities Source Ultimate** collection. It is published three times a year.

Subscription Rates:

Print edition: USD $30 per volume; USD $90 per year starting in 2015 (3 volumes).

Online edition: USD $101 per volume; USD $303 per year starting in 2015 (3 volumes).

The above prices include standard shipping. Confirm with seller for shipping costs in case of a special requirement or a remote territory.

How to subscribe:

Both print and online copies can also be purchased through the joint publishers:

1. Place orders directly with CLC Editorial Office

Jiang Sheng, CLC Global Subscriptions contact

Hotlines: +1 307 312 0714; +86 18022878796

Email and PayPal: zilinltd@icloud.com

WeChat & QQ: 1153692889

2. Buy individual copies through online bookstores:

Current volume and back volumes are available as hardcopy books and ebooks in Amazon, Barnes and Noble, and other major online retailing channels. In order to get the correct item, use keywords "Chinese Literature and Culture" and "Dongwei."

3. Buy cheap online editions through Magzter:

Individuals are strongly encouraged to subscribe through the online magazine portal MAGZTER, where it is very cheap to get CLC on your mobile devices.

Chinese Literature and Culture Subscription and Purchase Form
《中国文学与文化》征订单（编辑部美国代购）

As *Chinese Literature and Culture* is an academic journal with a limited readership, all subscriptions and purchases are fulfilled on print-on-demand basis and therefore are non-refundable. (因为《中国文学与文化》为小众学术期刊，根据订单数量定制印刷，暂无能力提供退货服务，谢谢支持。)

CLC Global Subscriptions (全球征订联络处):Hotlines (热线): +86 18022878796 +1 307 312 0714

Email (电子邮件及 PayPal 账号): zilinltd@icloud.com

Ms. Jiang, New Leaves Arts & Letters Lab, Zilin Limited Guangzhou, No. 5 Jinxi'erjie, Flat 211, Huaduqu, Guangzhou, 510890, China （联系人：广州市花都区金熙二街 211 房字林新叶文学艺术实验室蒋老师）

Year 年份	Rates, Print 纸质版年定价	Rates, Online 电子版年定价
2014	☐US$60 (2 vols)	☐US$202
2015	☐US$90 (3 vols)	☐US$303
2016	☐US$90 (3 vols)	☐US$303
2017	☐US$90 (3 vols)	☐US$303
2018	☐US$90 (3 vols)	☐US$303

Payment 支付:

☐PayPal: zilinltd@icloud.com （账号）, in the amount of US$_____ （美元金额）. Include payment record （请附支付记录）

☐**Please send my journal to** (请把所订杂志寄至)：

Name (联系人):_____

Address (地址):_____

Telephone （电话):_____Email (电子邮件):_____

Chinese Literature and Culture is simultaneously offered as a book series in online bookstores such as **Amazon, Barnes & Noble, IndieBound, Books-A-Million**, and other third party distribution channels. Search the ISBN in www.isbnsearch.org to see more channels that carry the titles.

Chinese Literature and Culture Volume 1
ISBN-13: 978-1502541963
ISBN-10: 1502541963

Chinese Literature and Culture Volume 2
ISBN-13: 978-1540894212
ISBN-10: 1540894215

Chinese Literature and Culture Volume 3
ISBN-13: 978-1514815182
ISBN-10: 1514815184

Chinese Literature and Culture Volume 4
ISBN-13: 978-1522836797
ISBN-10: 1522836799

Chinese Literature and Culture Volume 5: Xue Yiwei and His War Stories
ISBN-13: 978-1530443246;
ISBN-10: 1530443245

Chinese Literature and Culture Volume 6
ISBN-13: 978-1533095121;
ISBN-10: 1533095124

Chinese Literature and Culture Volume 6
ISBN-13: 978-1540739384
ISBN-10: 1540739384

Chinese Literature and Culture Volume 8
ISBN-13: 978-1542412438;
ISBN-10: 1542412439

Chinese Literature and Culture, Volume 8, December 2016
Chinese Literature and Culture is a **New Leaves**® journal jointly published by IntLingo Inc., Westbury, New York and Zilin Limited, Guangzhou. **New Leaves**® is a US imprint and trademark of Guangzhou Zilin Cultural Development Company Limited

Joint Publishers:

Publishing Division, IntLingo Inc.
400 Post Ave., Suite 305, Westbury, 11590, NY

New Leaves Arts & Letters Lab, Guangzhou Zilin Limited, Guangzhou
No. 5 Jinxi'erjie, Flat 211, Huaduqu, Guangzhou, 510890, China

Partners:
Hua Cheng magazine
School of Interpreting and Translation Studies, Guangdong University of Foreign Studies
Center for Translation Studies, Guangdong University of Foreign Studies

Chinese Literature and Culture Volume 8
ISSN: 2332-4287 (print)
ISSN: 2334-1122 (online)